032-02,

A Pointless History Of The World

Also By Alexander Armstrong And Richard Osman:

The 100 Most Pointless Things In The World
The 100 Most Pointless Arguments
In The World . . . Solved!
The Very Pointless Quiz Book
The A–Z Of Pointless

A Pointless History Of The World

Alexander Armstrong and Richard Osman

CORONET

First published in Great Britain in 2016 by Coronet
An imprint of Hodder & Stoughton
An Hachette UK company

1

Copyright © Alexander Armstrong, Richard Osman, Endemol 2016

The right of Alexander Armstrong, Richard Osman, Endemol to be identified
as the Authors of the Work has been asserted by them in accordance
with the Copyright, Designs and Patents Act 1988.

A CIP catalogue record for this title is available from the British Library

Hardback ISBN: 978 1 473 62323 1
Ebook ISBN: 978 1 473 62322 4

Typeset in Celeste 13/19pt by
Palimpsest Book Production Limited, Falkirk, Stirlingshire

Printed and bound by Clays Ltd, St Ives plc

Hodder &   that are natural
renewable a   for products and made from wood grown in
sustainable forest   to logging and manufacturing processes expected   to
conform to   environmental regulations of the country of origin.

CONTENTS

INTRODUCTION   1

1   The Big Bang   3

2   Dinosaurs   7

3   Cave Paintings   13

4   The Ice Age   19

5   Look Who's Talking   25

6   Did Aliens Ever Visit Us?   29

7   The Invention of Writing   35

8   The Invention of the Wheel   41

9   Mesopotamia   49

10 Egypt   53

11 When Did Different Animals Appear?   57

12 Stonehenge   65

13 Jesus   71

14 Jokes   75

15 The Fall of the Roman Empire   83

16 Anglo-Saxons, Vikings, Would Everybody
    Please Stop Invading?   89

17 London   97

18 Meanwhile, In Scotland   105

19 The Battle of Hastings   113

20 The Crusades   119

21 The Domesday Book   125

22 Bruce Forsyth   133

23	The Magna Carta	137
24	Black Death	143
25	The Peasants' Revolt	149
26	Wales	155
27	The Printing Press	163
28	Henry VIII, etc.	167
29	Spanish Armada	173
30	Shakespeare	177
31	The Gunpowder Plot	185
32	Galileo	191
33	The Great Fire of London	197
34	Newton's Cradle	205
35	Dr Johnson's *A Dictionary of the English Language* (1755)	209
36	American War of Independence	213
37	The Industrial Revolution	221
38	Napoleon	229
39	Stephenson's *Rocket* and the Rainhill Trials	235
40	Electricity	243
41	Nineteenth-century books	249
42	Telephone	255
43	Cars	263
44	Wright Brothers Fly	267
45	Television!	273
46	Churchill	281
47	1970	287
48	Pointless	293
49	Today	299
50	Tomorrow	305

INTRODUCTION

So, we learn a lot when we're making *Pointless*. To give you an example, one of the things we have learnt, and only very recently, is that when we have young professionals from the world of business on the show they like to start whatever they're saying with 'so'. So, we find this enormously impressive. Another thing we have picked up along the way is that there are some categories that people do less well in than others. Current affairs is one. Moons of Jupiter is another, but the biggie is history. Again and again history is where our brave contestants come unseated like little jockeys on our tea-time race-track. The Stuarts? *Crash*! The War of the Roses? *skid noise* *Smash*! British Prime Ministers? *skid noise* *Kerpow*! *noise of horse shoe rolling off and clattering, but on grass so probably quite quietly*.

So, our lovely publishers thought it was time we took our usual book format of quiz-questions-interspersed-with-things-we want-to-talk-about (and blimey, have we covered some subjects these past five years: pub decorations, disappointing zoo animals, who our 100 people are) and used it to address the issue of history head-on.

So, we have taken the history of the universe, weighed it

up, rolled it around in our hands, and then popped it back down on the bar. Sorry, desk – *definitely* desk. We have truffled out the 50 most important focus points on an (admittedly) Earth-biased history timeline and provided an accessible hop-on, hop-off tour around these points. Oh and also we've put in lots of *Pointless* quiz questions. So, this means you have everything you need between these two covers to hold your very own *Pointless* tournament (including the answers and complete score breakdowns) and to become enormously knowledgeable in all fields of history.

So. So what are you waiting for?

1
THE BIG BANG

Where better to start our history of the world than at the very beginning, the Big Bang?

Occurring around 13.8 billion years ago, the Big Bang was so named because it was *really* loud and *really* big.

It was so loud that if it happened next door while you were watching *EastEnders* you would knock on the wall and tell your neighbours to keep the noise down. It was officially noisier than when someone in the *Pointless* audience tries to open sweets and thinks we won't notice.

It was so big that if it wore shoes it wouldn't be able to buy them in regular shoe shops, but would have to get them online from America.

Scientists believe that the universe went through more changes during its first second than in the entirety of the 13.8 billion years that followed. The first six great epochs of the universe all occurred within that first second. Scientists would agree that in this way it is similar to an episode of *Pointless* when someone on the first podium gets a pointless answer, and then we don't get another one for the rest of the show.

What we do know is that within that first second every atom in the universe was born. Therefore, without this first second we wouldn't now have many things that are very important to *Pointless*, including the Central African Republic, Rutherfordium and Greg Rusedski.

Of course one of the great philosophical and scientific questions of our time is 'what happened before the Big Bang?' As it happens I have worked out the answer to this question, but as this book is *The Pointless History Of The World*, there is no place to include it here. Instead I will cover it in my next book, *The Naughty Monkey Who Burped the Universe*, which I am co-writing with Chico.

STEPHEN HAWKING

Here are five clues to facts about the physicist Stephen Hawking. Please work out the answer you think the fewest of our 100 people knew.

He was born on the 300th anniversary of the death of this scientist

Mathematician with whom he co-wrote *The Nature of Space and Time*

Title of his best-selling 1988 popular science book

US animated TV series he first appeared in, in 1999

US state he took a zero-gravity flight from in 2007

GALILEO GALILEI 3

SIR ROGER PENROSE 1

A BRIEF HISTORY OF TIME 17

THE SIMPSONS 41

FLORIDA 11

2
DINOSAURS

And BOOM, that's how I discover about Chico. Of course, it was only a matter of time before someone younger and more energetic caught Richard's collaborative eye. But how long has everyone known? How long – I want to know – have I been living on Chico time?

You see that's the thing about extinction, isn't it? It's an accident waiting to happen as far as everyone else is concerned. We can all see a mile off why extinct things (the Great auk, the Sabre-toothed cat, BHS) ended up going the way of the – well, actually, there we go: the Dodo is an excellent example. Look at it with its lovely silly face, its stupid great bulbous beak-end and funny fringe. It's the poster creature for extinction, the cute butt of one of nature's cruellest jokes: an animal whose lot in life was to be flightless and, at the same time, delicious.*

---

* And by putting the words 'cute' and 'butt' next to each other I have guaranteed the online version of this book an extra 13.5 million hits.

It's like the car that pulls out right in front of you with a left-hand panel full of dents: its markings tell you everything you need to know. Or like the hilarious warning on bottles of hair tonic† that tell you to wash your hands immediately after use for fear that otherwise great tussocks of hair might start sprouting FROM YOUR VERY HANDS, so science-bustingly potent (and yet curiously unacknowledged) is the preparation therein. You might as well print a spangly star on the packaging with the words 'Never bought twice!'

But dinosaurs. Dinosaurs! So long extinct, and blending so seamlessly with the flying broomsticks and never-ending porridge pots of make-believe that it's hard to picture them actually lolling about on Earth 200 million years ago, chewing on their legs, swatting away flies, farting in the sun. But loll they did, and *everywhere*; their remains are dotted around from Argentina to Cardiff (like James Dean Bradfield's missing socks). When I was little I only really knew about the Tyrannosaurus Rex and – largely thanks to a top-forty hit of the same name by the generously tongued naturalist David Bellamy – the Brontosaurus, but there were of course countless thousands of species of dinosaur that didn't really get much attention in the pre-Michael Crichton '70s. Dinosaurs were around for 135 million years. So far we, *Homo erectus*, have clocked up a mere two million. It feels a bit like only the second day of half-term and everyone's already getting a bit fractious –

† Apparently.

how the hell are we going to keep it together for the next 133 million years?

Dinosaurs, even towards the end of their stint, were fairly ridiculous creatures though. I think we can agree on that, can't we? Why, for example, were they so enormous? What was the thinking behind that, I wonder? And how did it come about? It's an evolutionary model that was quietly dropped in the next round of developments almost as if there were two completely different – and competing – evolutionary strands: one that has led to the emergence of small, agile, creatures with thumbs that can make gravy and set up a legislature to protect newts, and the other which led to roaring creatures the size of modest tower-blocks with massive teeth and horns and little baby arms (again, you'll have to forgive the occasional *tiny* gap in my dinosaur knowledge here). I'm afraid, evolutionarily speaking (if I can speak like that, and you know what, I've just tried it and I CAN), I get a modest kick out of what we have achieved in our comparatively short time here. (I've never seen the remains of any dinosaur accordions or dinosaur Mr Blobby Worlds – and they were here for *135 million years.* What were they doing?) Now I know that not everything is a competition, but I just like the fact that we have (at the time of publication) kind of won. Haven't we? Obviously that isn't entirely down to our dexterity, agility and intelligence so much as to the unscheduled arrival of a sizeable chunk of space rock. But it doesn't alter the fact that we, the pathetic little bipeds in this fight, totally *own* the dinosaurs. Evolutionarily speaking. So nah.

Exactly where this leaves me *vis-à-vis* Chico, though, I'm not entirely sure.

We are looking for the title of any single by T. Rex that reached the Top 40 in the UK chart, according to the Official Charts Company. We will accept Double A-sides as separate answers. For the purposes of this question we are including singles that were released under the names 'Tyrannosaurus Rex' or 'Marc Bolan & T. Rex' as well.

20TH CENTURY BOY	8
CHILDREN OF THE REVOLUTION	2
DEBORA	0
DREAMY LADY	0
GET IT ON	8
HOT LOVE	3
I LOVE TO BOOGIE	2
JEEPSTER	1
LIGHT OF LOVE	0
LONDON BOYS	0
METAL GURU	9
NEW YORK CITY	0
ONE INCH ROCK	0
RIDE A WHITE SWAN	19
SOLID GOLD EASY ACTION	0
TEENAGE DREAM	0
TELEGRAM SAM	2
THE GROOVER	0
TRUCK ON (TYKE)	0

3
CAVE PAINTINGS

The first of our human ancestors – *Homo erectus* – emerged in Africa somewhere between one and two million years ago. They were, of course, very primitive and lacked even basic human characteristics such as owning Soda Streams and Sky Plus.

Archaeologists in Kenya, going even further back than that, have uncovered rudimentary tools fashioned over 3.3 million years ago, almost certainly by the ape-like *Australopithecus*. The 'tools' were rocks fashioned into rudimentary hammers, cutting blades and anvils. If you want to know how the archaeologists could distinguish these rocks from other regular rocks, it's because they all still had their barcodes on them.

For hundreds of thousands of years many different types of human-like species co-existed, most famously the Neanderthals, the first remains of which were discovered in 1856 in Germany's Neander Valley. They had short, strong limbs, made stone and bone tools and very much enjoyed watching *The Chase*.

But it wasn't until around 30,000 years ago that *Homo sapiens* – that's us, you, me, Keith Chegwin, Atomic Kitten, everyone – became the only surviving human species, and we've had humanity to ourselves ever since.

The most lasting achievement from this era is cave paintings, many of which survive to this day. The earliest verified example is found in a cave on the Indonesian island of Sulawesi. It is a painting of a babirusa, a pig-deer creature, and at over 35,000 years old it is the first picture in the history of the world. This, don't forget, was some 34,993 years before the invention of Instagram.

Most of the early cave paintings to have been discovered – from Indonesia, to famous examples in France and Spain, to countless others from Somalia, Algeria and elsewhere – are remarkably similar paintings of animals. No-one can quite agree why the paintings in wildly different cultures painted thousands of years apart should be so similar in form and subject. It is thought by many that animals perhaps had a religious or shamanic significance which transcended borders. However, if I were in charge of research into this I would just assume that they all liked drawing animals in exactly the same way we all enjoy watching cat videos on YouTube. 'Dude, have you seen the babirusa painting in Dave's cave?! Megalolz!'

Sometimes *Pointless* viewers ask me what I'm writing down with my ever-present pen. Well, during the bits of recordings where I have nothing to do, such as during the head-to-head deliberations, or when Xander is talking to someone about their allotment, I doodle a lot on my answer sheets. I sometimes like to imagine that those cave painters of 35,000 years ago are looking approvingly over my shoulder and whispering, 'Well done, Richard, that's a really good picture of a horse.'

CHARACTERS FROM ASTERIX

The correct answers on this list are all characters featured in the English translations of the 'Asterix the Gaul' series of books, written by Goscinny and Uderzo; the wrong answers have never appeared in the Asterix books. Can you find the correct answer the fewest of our 100 said?

ALCOHOLIX

VITALSTATISTIX

PREFIX

OBELIX

JUSTFORKIX

DOGMATIX

OMNITRIX

ALCOHOLIX	0
OMNITRIX	WRONG
DOGMATIX	7
JUSTFORKIX	1
OBELIX	24
PREFIX	0
VITALSTATISTIX	4

THE ICE AGE

Here's something I never knew until last year when I went to visit the Arctic Circle: GLACIERS COME FROM THE SKY. Why didn't anyone tell me that? It would have completely changed Geography for me. No-one (and I'm looking at you, Mr Burkinshaw) ever told me how hulking great rivers of slow-moving ice came to be on the land. I just imagined they bubbled up somehow, maybe from frozen seas. Or out of frozen springs. I don't know, this kind of stuff was given on a need-to-know basis clearly, and we only concerned ourselves with what was left behind by the glaciers rather than with the glaciers themselves. Did everyone else know about the glaciers? Was it meant to be obvious? The good news is that, aged forty-five, I found out and now it all makes perfect sense: they come from the – well, you'll have got the gist by now.

It's very simple. You just have to imagine what would happen if the temperature never rose above freezing – like, ever – so that all the rain fell as snow or hail and that it never melted (because it wouldn't, would it?) from season to season. Obviously to start with we'd be cheerful and we'd dress up in our woollens and clear paths in the ice and chat good-humouredly over the garden fence in misty clouds of hot breath as we did our gritting and shovelling and whatever, waiting for it all to melt. After a bit we'd just go inside, make some hot chocolate, light the fire and watch *Pointless*, and still not really worry about it. Then, for year after year after year, the unmelted snow from the previous years would be compacted by the weight of fresh snowfall, and the level of the ice on the ground would rise (quite handy to start with as it would make the telly room nice and dark, although sadly it would also eventually start to obscure that brilliant snowman you built fourteen years ago). And after, let's say, a hundred years, there'd be quite a thick crust of compacted snow (getting out of the front door would now be a challenge). Imagine this going on for thousands and thousands of years and you begin to get the idea of how huge volumes of compacted ice start to build up.

After a bit (and in this context a 'bit' is roughly equal to fifty millennia – by now the *Pointless* episodes on Challenge are starting to look a little tired) the sheer weight of the ice mass forces it to move, sometimes in directions guided by the geological robustness of the rock formations beneath it (and whether or not you went for double glazing in the telly room), sometimes due to the unevenness of the weight distribution.

That – in very broad terms – is what happens during an ice age. How ice ages come about, however, is another thing Mr Burkinshaw forgot to tell me, and on this occasion I didn't learn about it in the Arctic Circle either, so you'll have to look it up in a heavy book.

Or ask Richard.

WINTER OLYMPIC LOCATION

We are looking for any country in which the Winter Olympics have taken place, up to and including the 2014 Games.

We are looking for the name of the country as it is currently known.

And of course by 'country' we mean the current usual English name of any sovereign state that is a member of the UN.

AUSTRIA	27
BOSNIA AND HERZEGOVINA	2
CANADA	58
FRANCE	31
GERMANY	16
ITALY	22
JAPAN	23
NORWAY	24
RUSSIA	65
SWITZERLAND	32
USA	40

5
LOOK WHO'S TALKING

The development of language is possibly the single weirdest, most unlikely, most extraordinary and most significant event in the whole of human history. It is so deeply, irredeemably odd and bewilderingly magnificent.

Some linguists believe language sprang into being due to a chance mutation, but most think it developed, very slowly, over many, many thousands of years.

They are fairly certain that our good friends *Australopithecus* had no system of language. Which meant when they were in B&Q buying their hammers and anvils, they either simply had to point, or they had to use the self-service checkouts.

Possibly as far back as 2.3 million years ago, primitive language systems developed, but it wasn't until around sixty to a hundred thousand years ago that the age of spoken language systems as we might understand them began to emerge. It allowed Stone Age estate agents, disc jockeys and broadband support telephone operatives to thrive, but also brought many good things too.

So how did it develop? Well, no-one really knows, but I have developed a theory. Before the development of language, Scrabble was simply two people looking at a board waiting for something to happen. This led me to think that maybe language was actually developed by a Scrabble player endlessly and systematically cheating. After playing the letters 'ROCK', for example, her opponent would naturally shrug and challenge the word. She would then point at something nearby – in this case a rock – and put her thumbs up. Thus, over a series of say twenty to thirty games the basics of human language were invented. Further credence is given to this theory when you consider that the letters C and V are the hardest to get rid of in Scrabble, and one of the first words was, rather conveniently, 'cave'.

If language had not been invented, *Pointless* as we know it today would be very different. After the theme tune you'd simply see Xander smiling and waving. He'd then point to the contestants, each of whom would do an elaborate mime to tell us they were a baker from Huddersfield, or a university admissions administrator from Bangor, North Wales. At this point Xander would look over at me and I'd panic as I realised that round one was supposed to be 'Words ending in . . . ARK'.

Tipping Point would be largely unaffected.

LANGUAGE

We are going to give you fourteen French names for countries. Can you work out what their English translations are?

ALLEMAGNE

CHYPRE

ÉRYTHRÉE

ESPAGNE

ÉTATS-UNIS

LETTONIE

LIBAN

MAROC

MAURICE

PAYS-BAS

POLOGNE

ROYAUME-UNI

SAINT-MARIN

SUÈDE

GERMANY	67
CYPRUS	56
ERITREA	11
SPAIN	95
UNITED STATES	49
LATVIA	5
LEBANON	7
MOROCCO	43
MAURITIUS	15
NETHERLANDS	26
POLAND	66
UNITED KINGDOM	37
SAN MARINO	13
SWEDEN	64

6
DID ALIENS EVER VISIT US?

There is a theory which suggests that Earth was visited by alien intelligences a number of times during the course of ancient history, and that these events help to explain many developments of early humanity. Of course, there are many theories about many things – Xander is still adamant for example that Timothy Dalton was the best James Bond – but let's hear this one out.

How were the pyramids built? How could the massive stones of Stonehenge possibly have been transported? Who was responsible for the extraordinary Moai statues on Easter Island?

Now, you and I might believe that the answer to all of the above was a combination of mass slavery and people having an awful lot of time on their hands when there were no box sets of *Breaking Bad* to watch.

But the theories of alien visitation, most famously outlined by Erich von Däniken in *Chariots of the Gods*, point to lots of other evidence.

Cave paintings and artefacts from around the world often appear to show flying saucers or unusual objects in the sky. How to explain this? Well, fridge-door paintings done by my children when they were young appear to show that the sun is green and that I have some sort of a Mohican, but this is not evidence that either of those things is true. Some people are just bad at drawing. Not me, as anyone who has ever seen my horse doodles will attest.

(On a side note, it seems to me that 'Horse Doodles' would be a very bad name for a restaurant.)

But it is certainly true that at various points in human history enormous technological advances seemed to take place all at once. How can we explain this without positing some sort of external influence was involved? Well here's the thing: there has never been a time of greater techno-logical and societal change in the whole of human history than the last 300 years. We often imagine ourselves to be at the pinnacle of history, but in this regard we are. And we know that the developments of the last 300 years weren't due to alien invention. They were due to James Watt and Steve Wozniak, to Katharine Blodgett and the Wright Brothers, to whoever invented those keys that beep when you whistle and the genius behind the Mint Viennetta.

Without the last 300 years the only questions on *Pointless* would be 'The Wives of Henry VIII', 'The Seven Ancient

Wonders of the World' and 'The Last Time Arsenal Won the Premier League'.

It seems a virtual certainty that intelligent alien life forms have never visited Earth, but far from certain that they never will. The theory of 'Panspermia' suggests that the building blocks of life have existed everywhere in the universe since the Big Bang, and it is only a matter of time before we discover we are not alone.

(On a final note, it occurs to me that 'Panspermia' would be an even worse name for a restaurant.)

ALIEN RACES

The correct answers here are all fictional, non-human races from sci-fi TV or film. The incorrect answers will not be names of alien races. Can you pick the lowest correct answer?

CONEHEADS

GROCKLES

KLINGONS

KOTTO

MYSTERONS

NIBBLONIANS

SPACEBALLS

Coneheads	1	From the US film *Coneheads* based on a *Saturday Night Live* comedy sketch.
Grockles	WRONG	Incorrect, this is not an alien race, but rather an informal term meaning 'tourists' – used in some parts of the UK – particularly used for domestic tourists from other parts of the UK.
Klingons	45	From *Star Trek*.
Kotto	WRONG	Incorrect, this is not an alien race. Yaphet Kotto was an actor in the 1979 film *Alien* – played 'Parker', the ship's chief engineer.
Mysterons	3	From *Captain Scarlet and the Mysterons*.
Nibblonians	0	From Matt Groening's *Futurama*. Three-eyed and voracious – they look cute and cuddly, but will eat anything that moves. They are from the planet Eternium at the exact centre of the universe.
Spaceballs	0	From the planet Spaceball in the 1987 Mel Brooks film *Spaceballs*.

7

THE INVENTION OF WRITING

The earliest surviving example of a human being writing something down in symbols was found among the remains of the ancient civilisation of Sumer in Southern Mesopotamia and has been dated to an era 5,200 years ago (that's two whole years before the release of 'Move It' by Cliff Richard). This area of Mesopotamia is what people often refer to (rather beautifully) as the Cradle of Civilisation. These days, of course, Mesopotamia is not a sovereign state in its own right that is recognised by the UN, but roughly speaking it is an area now covered by Syria, Iraq and Kuwait (so not especially news-worthy) and was the site of humankind's first urbanised civilisation. The Mesopotamians drained the marshes for agriculture and established basic industries (pottery, leather, masonry and sequin work – I'm pretty sure that's right) and set up a trading base. But most importantly, as the discovery of these tiny carved symbols demonstrates, they 'invented' writing. They were the first people ever to put down marks whose meaning another person could understand. Wow. Seriously, wow. How cool to be able to leave messages on bits of rock, instead of having to hang around saying, 'Caution, cleaning in process – floor may be slippery' to every single person who walks past.

Unsurprisingly, the Sumerian sample is basic but the primitive hieroglyph follows a repetitive canon that is not without sophistication. We are introduced to two characters: 'Fox' and 'Companion'. From the second system on, the Companion is pictured as a dog or goat although it's not always consistent. The agile Fox, elaborately coloured with burnt umber to show his lustrous brown fur, jumps over the recumbent Companion or Dog. This motif is then repeated fifty times.

Also discovered in Sumer – and dating from only a century or so after the tableaux above – was a series of clay tablets on which were written the first ever work of literature. Not a tale of kings and battles but an epic saga about the wife of a Ubaidian farmer, who is bored at home one day until a delivery man appears with a parcel for next door.

OLOGIES

When the suffix 'ology' is added to a prefix, it often gives the title for a field of study. Audiology, for example, is the study of hearing. Can you name the fields of study from the words supplied? We're looking for one-word answers for each of these 'ologies'.

CAMPANOLOGY

CHROMATOLOGY

CONCHOLOGY

GRAPHOLOGY

HAEMATOLOGY

HIPPOLOGY

ICHTHYOLOGY

BELLS   53

COLOURS   24

SHELLS   21

HANDWRITING   27

BLOOD   69

HORSES   13

FISH   11

OLOGIES

- OENOLOGY
- ORNITHOLOGY
- OSTEOLOGY
- SEISMOLOGY
- SINOLOGY
- TRICHOLOGY
- VEXILLOLOGY

WINES   9

BIRDS   58

BONES   36

EARTHQUAKES   53

CHINA   11

HAIR   22

FLAGS   3

8

THE INVENTION OF
THE WHEEL

One of the strange and wonderful things about human history is how almost identical ideas have frequently taken root simultaneously in completely different parts of the world. Confucius and Socrates, for example, were alive at the same time, one in China and the other in Ancient Greece. All right, Confucius died when Socrates was only five, but still, there they were on their opposite sides of the planet channelling very much the same kinds of ideas on morality, principles of government and favourite milk-shake recipes. What was the charge that caused these sparks to fly at that precise moment? Was it something in the air? Or had the human population simply reached a level that started to require structure and governance for the first time? Who knows why these things come about . . .

When *Pointless* was being developed and run out for its

first series in the safety of BBC 2's afternoon programme nursery, a new show in Australia called *How Much Do You Know Ya F***ing Galah?* was simultaneously getting its tentative first airing on Australian TV. *HMDYKYFG* has since become a cornerstone of the schedules in both Australia and New Zealand. And while there was absolutely no cross-over in the two programmes' development, they share a striking number of similarities. I do occasionally wonder if the Jimmy Pell who runs Pelmanism Productions in Melbourne is the same Jimmy Pell who used to work in the Walkabout in Shepherd's Bush where we regularly went for drinks after our production meetings, but, given his track record on other hit shows in Australia,* I'm inclined to think it's just 'something in the air'.

I mention all this because the invention of the wheel – that often-cited moment in human evolution – seems to be something no-one can really pin down to one particular place or even one particular time. The wheel just seems to have appeared like a smell or a Beyoncé album and prolif-erated. The earliest evidence of wheeled transport being in use dates from the fourth century BC, but discoveries from the same period have been found in many different places – in the south of modern-day Russia, modern-day Moldova and in our old friend Sumer in Mesopotamia.

How did the invention come about? There is a school of thought that says the wheel is an extraordinarily special development for early Bronze Age civilisations, on account

* *Which Box is the Bloody Money In?* and *One of These Bast**ds is Lying.*

of the fact that the wheel doesn't appear in nature, but I wonder about that. Nature is *lifting* with wheel clues: round rocks that roll down hills, snowballs that roll – again – down hills (yes, Sumer may not have had much by way of snow but its neighbour, Wynter, had bags of the stuff), round fruits and nuts that roll, tree trunks that roll and that, like the banana, when cut into thin cross-sections – hey presto! – are kind of proto-wheels. Once a month the night sky gives us a clue with its perfect lunar wheel. And then, back in the cave store cupboard, Maltesers, Polos, Wagon Wheels . . . oh yes, no-one say nature was being coy when it came to wheel hints.

I suppose what is significant is that our ancestors had arrived at the point where they had the constructive imagination to take the wheel as an idea and adapt it with an axle. This was the moment when we started to pull away from our fellow grunters in the animal kingdom and establish ourselves as the fancy dans of evolution.

INVENTIONS

We're going to give you descriptions of inventions which have improved day-to-day living during the 19th and 20th centuries. We've given you the initials of the invention in brackets. Please tell us what the letters stand for. As ever, you are looking for the answer the fewest of our 100 people knew.

A cooling cabinet for preserving food (R)

A double-walled vessel used to keep food hot or cold (VF)

A fastening device consisting of 2 parallel rows of teeth interlocked by a sliding tab (Z)

A near-instant cooker patented by Percy Spencer in 1945 (MO)

A small pouch, originally made from silk, containing leaves that make a beverage (TB)

Alloy mainly of iron and chromium that resists corrosion (SS)

Device which sprays regulated amount of fuel into a car engine where it is combusted (C)

REFRIGERATOR   38

VACUUM FLASK   42

ZIP   91

MICROWAVE OVEN   64

TEA BAG   88

STAINLESS STEEL   70

CARBURETTOR   34

INVENTIONS

Fibre introduced as a silk-substitute in 1938 used in the manufacture of stockings (N)

Item used for shaving containing a guard and removable blade (SR)

Length of wire coiled into a spring with a point at one end and clasp at the other (SP)

Machine for cleaning crockery, shown at the Chicago World's Fair in 1893 (D)

Metal food wrapping material that forms a protective barrier (AF)

Waterproof, wipe-clean floor covering made from linseed oil (L)

Weaving machine that used punched cards to produce intricate patterns (JL)

NYLON	79
SAFETY RAZOR	24
SAFETY PIN	4
DISHWASHER	89
ALUMINIUM FOIL	60
LINOLEUM	39
JACQUARD LOOM	1

MESOPOTAMIA

It is far from an exaggeration to say that much of what you know and much of who you are comes from one place: Mesopotamia.

Mesopotamia, 'the land between the rivers', covered the area between the rivers Tigris and Euphrates, what is now broadly modern-day Iraq, and was quite simply the Cradle of Western Civilisation.

So many of the things that define our modern world were either invented, or underwent transformational change, in this one small area many thousands of years ago. The wheel, cursive script, cereal crops, mathematics, philosophy, libraries, astronomy and so much else grew and thrived in this extraordinary area. Without the Mesopotamians we wouldn't have Monster Trucks, Cereal Cafés in Shoreditch or double maths on Wednesday afternoon. Things that the Mesopotamians didn't invent include reality TV, rounds about golf on *Pointless*, and your work colleagues constantly going on about how they are no longer eating Twixes because they are training for a triathlon and then expecting you to sponsor them.

Allow me to digress for a moment. We recently had a round on *Pointless* where contestants had to fill in blanks on a board of historical locations, and one of the clues was yet another of the countless achievements of the Mesopotamians:

THE HANGING _ _ _ _ _ _ _ OF BABYLON

This caused no trouble in the studio but I just want to note that one of our 100 answered 'Baskets'.

Moving swiftly on. You are also probably *from* Mesopotamia. Up to 80 per cent of modern Europeans can trace their ancestry back to farmers who left modern-day Iraq and Syria 10,000 years ago. Which leads me to a conclusion of sorts. What a wonderful, smart, beautiful, interconnected gang the human race truly is. We are all just a blink in history, but that history is shared by us all, and we all sit around the same campfire telling the same stories.

And wherever we are, there's always one of us who thinks it was 'The Hanging Baskets of Babylon'.

ANCIENT CITIES

We're going to give you some facts, each of which relates to a different Ancient City. We would like you to tell us the names of the Ancient Cities from the clues.

According to legend, a giant, wooden horse was dragged through its gate

Capital of southern Mesopotamia famous for its hanging gardens

Inca city standing at 2,340 metres above sea-level

Now in modern Jordan, used as a film location for *Indiana Jones and the Last Crusade*

Seaport of Ancient Rome that stood at the mouth of the River Tiber

TROY	69
BABYLON	59
MACHU PICCHU	26
PETRA	11
OSTIA	4

EGYPT

So Mesopotamia gets 'the Cradle of Civilisation', which is nice. 'Cradle', as I said earlier, is poetic; it's where we're nurtured, where we grow, where we're cared for. I like the idea of early civilisation being tended, fed and gently burped. I'm not going to take anything away from what was happening down there between the Tigris and the Euphrates because those guys were unquestionably terrific. Cradle of Civilisation? Help yourself! But where does that leave Egypt? What have we got left in our little name larder for them? Egypt did plenty of heavy lifting in the infancy of civilisation. Have we got a nice name for them? What's that? We haven't? Oops. That's awkward. It's like we've called James Brown 'The Godfather of Soul' and we've somehow forgotten to give Clyde McPhatter a name. What's that? Who's Clyde McPhatter? Well that's my point – McPhatter is unequivocally a closer relation of Soul than Brown. What exactly was Brown's role in relation to Soul? A godfather?

I mean, at best that's probably just someone who went to college with Soul's dad and forgets its birthdays every year.

Egypt had a number of small tribes living in it by 5500 BC. The Nile, with its regular flooding, fertile valley and glorious delta by which it flowed into the Mediterranean, proved perfect territory for a people to start learning all about agriculture. And learn they did – they worked out that they could ride the unpredictable nature of the Nile's ebbs and flows by building water-storage facilities and sophisticated irrigation channels. The Egyptians were the first people to move civilisation away from subsistence farming, whereby everyone worked full time growing and hunting what they could to support themselves, to a system of centralised farming, whereby 'farmers' were in charge of providing food for everyone and the individual citizens could get on with Maths, Building, Jewellery Making, Procreating, Astronomy, Squash Club, Fencing or Outward Bound.* This – make no mistake – was a massive leap forward, as it led to a huge and almost embarrassingly productive population who were capable of phenomenal feats of engineering, writing, building and orienteering across Dartmoor.

So can we all agree in the future to think like this: Mesopotamia: Cradle of Civilisation; Egypt: Civilisation's Older Brother's Friend from School?

* OB not available in the Christmas Term.

ARCHAEOLOGY

We are going to give you five clues to facts about archaeology, archaeologists or fictional archaeologists. We would like you to tell us the answer to the clue you think the fewest of our 100 people knew.

Archaeologist who led the team that discovered Tutankhamun's tomb in 1922

Fictional archaeologist played by Harrison Ford in *Raiders of the Lost Ark*

The Suffolk Anglo-Saxon ship burial site uncovered in 1939

This Inca citadel in Peru was rediscovered by Hiram Bingham in 1911

Video game franchise about the archaeologist adventurer Lara Croft

HOWARD CARTER 14

INDIANA JONES 39

SUTTON HOO 15

MACHU PICCHU 22

TOMB RAIDER 65

WHEN DID DIFFERENT ANIMALS APPEAR?

How many years ago did the following animals appear?

620 million: The very first animals, the Ediacarans. They were a bit like sponges and would have made boring pets, albeit fairly easy to look after.

550 million: Marine life began to thrive, with the emergence of worms, molluscs, jellyfish and coral. I know that coral is really millions of tiny animals but I don't actually *believe* it. I mean, if you asked me what coral really is I would reply 'Well, it's just some coral, isn't it?' That's why I'm not an animal scientist.

530 million: The first ever footprints are found on land. Made by a big centipede, which I suppose is how they managed to spot the footprints.

500 million: The first fish, including relatives of fish such as lungfish and carp. And given that a goldfish is a type of carp, then I'm going to say that goldfish are essentially 500 million years old.

450 million: Sharks. Okay, now we're really talking. Shortly after the emergence of the first shark the Discovery Channel was launched.

420 million: Spiders. One of the first land creatures. There was one spider, the Slimonia, which was a relative of the scorpion and the size of a human being. I can't be the only person wondering who would win in a fight between a shark and a Slimonia.

320 million: Lizards, which of course led to dinosaurs, which in turn led to *Jurassic Park*, which in turn led to *Jurassic Park: The Lost World*, which led in turn to *Jurassic Park III*, which led in turn to *Jurassic World*. In case Xander hasn't already covered these important developments under 'Dinosaurs'.

125 million: Kangaroos. Well, marsupials anyway. Not actually kangaroos, but it's fun to think of kangaroos hanging out with dinosaurs.

70 million: Parrots.

60 million: The first primate. A kind of lemur, like a tree-dwelling Joey Essex.

55 million: Cows and pigs and horses. Fifty-five million years ago was a big time for animals.

40 million: Whales. After 390 million years as the coolest thing in the sea, sharks must have been all like 'WTF???'

35 million: Rabbits. They bred so quickly it's hard to think of a metaphor to describe it.

30 million: 'Leman's Dawn Cat' was the first true cat. We can tell it was the first true cat because it would always sit on Leman's paper as he was trying to read it.

25 million: Meerkats. And so car insurance was born.

40,000: The very first domesticated dogs. Though in dog years that's actually 280,000 years ago. Nothing much changed with dogs until 1955 when someone invented the Labradoodle and the Cockapoo. I say 'invented', you know how this works.

25: About twenty-five years ago someone developed the micropig. I only mention this because of the amount of people, Paris Hilton included, who bought micropigs as pets only to discover that they had actually just bought baby pigs and they continued to grow to full size, with the original seller long disappeared. Which is about as neat a way to sum up 620 million years of evolution as I can imagine.

ANIMAL ACTS

We are going to give you a list of four music acts that all have an animal in their name. We'd like you simply to name a top 40 UK single by any of them, according to the Official Charts Company. We are including collaborations with other named artists. This is up to the beginning of October 2012. Both titles on a Double A-side single count separately. We are not accepting the titles of EPs.

ADAM AND THE ANTS/ADAM ANT

THE EAGLES

THE PUSSYCAT DOLLS

SNOOP DOGG

ADAM AND THE ANTS/ADAM ANT

ANT RAP	3
ANTMUSIC	14
APOLLO 9	0
CARTROUBLE	0
DESPERATE BUT NOT SERIOUS	0
DEUTSCHER GIRLS	0
DOG EAT DOG	2
FRIEND OR FOE	1
GOODY TWO SHOES	5
KINGS OF THE WILD FRONTIER	4
PRINCE CHARMING	47
PUSS 'N' BOOTS	1
ROOM AT THE TOP	0
STAND AND DELIVER	32
WONDERFUL	0
YOUNG PARISIANS	0

THE EAGLES

HEARTACHE TONIGHT	0
HOTEL CALIFORNIA	51
LYIN' EYES	4
NEW KID IN TOWN	2

ONE OF THESE NIGHTS	4
PLEASE COME HOME FOR CHRISTMAS	0
TAKE IT TO THE LIMIT	1

THE PUSSYCAT DOLLS

BEEP	0
DON'T CHA	27
HUSH HUSH	2
I DON'T NEED A MAN	1
I HATE THIS PART	0
JAI HO!	1
STICKWITU	2
WHATCHA THINK ABOUT THAT	0
WHEN I GROW UP	2

THE PUSSYCAT DOLLS/SNOOP DOGG

BUTTONS	3

SNOOP DOGG

BEAUTIFUL	1
CALIFORNIA GURLS	0
DOGGY DOGG WORLD	0
DROP IT LIKE IT'S HOT	1

FROM THA CHUUUCH TO DA PALACE	0
GIN AND JUICE	4
HOLIDAE IN	0
I WANNA LOVE YOU	0
I WANNA THANK YOU	0
LET'S GET BLOWN	0
SENSUAL SEDUCTION	0
SIGNS	0
SNOOP DOGG	0
SNOOPS UPSIDE YA HEAD	0
STILL DRE	0
SWEAT (WET)	0
THA DOGGFATHER	0
THAT'S THAT	0
THE MACK	0
THE NEXT EPISODE	0
UPS & DOWNS	0
VAPORS	0
WANTED DEAD OR ALIVE	0
WE JUST WANNA TO PARTY WITH YOU	0
WHAT'S MY NAME?	0
X	0

12
STONEHENGE

I have decided to write some of these entries with no reference whatsoever to any source material or research, in much the same way as I answered my O-Level English essay about H. E. Bates's *Fair Stood the Wind for France* without ever actually having read the book.

Let's start with Stonehenge, which I'm guessing I must know lots about.

Stonehenge is a series of 'stones' arranged in a 'henge' formation. You can see Stonehenge out of your right-hand window if you are driving to the West Country, and out of your left-hand window if you are driving in the other direction. No-one knows why this is, though some scholars believe it was designed by the Druids to get as many passing motorists to visit the gift shop as possible.

In the gift shop I bet you can buy tea towels with 'Stonehenge' written on them, as well as models of Stonehenge, books about Stonehenge, and a selection of confectionery and soft drinks. There are also almost certainly very good toilet facilities. I think I read there is now a Visitor Centre there too. That would certainly make a lot of sense.

Stonehenge is well ancient. How old is it exactly? Try this experiment. Think of how old *you* reckon Stonehenge is. Have you thought of a number? Well, get ready for a surprise: you are exactly right! The age you thought of is the age that Stonehenge is. You got it on your first guess.

The stones of Stonehenge are arranged in groups of three, with two 'supporters' and one 'balancer'. If we say there are maybe six of these groups at Stonehenge, that means there are eighteen stones in all. Though maybe they don't all have 'balancers'; I am trying to picture it in my mind. What we can say pretty much for certain is that there are something between fourteen and twenty-five stones at Stonehenge.

But the big mystery is where did these stones come from and how did they get to the place where Stonehenge is, which I think is near Salisbury? The answers are that the stones came from off the side of mountains, and the Druids ordered them from Ocado. The stones were supposed to be granite but Ocado had run out and offered these slightly more boring stones as replacements.

So that's Stonehenge. In other news, I got a B in my O-Level English.

INFLUENTIAL PLACES IN HISTORY

Here are fourteen clues to places that featured in *Time Magazine*'s list of the 'Most Influential Places in History', published in April 2012. Can you name these influential places?

To clarify, these places may be countries, buildings, cities etc.

A bank founded in Frankfurt, Germany, in 1998

A prehistoric stone circle near Amesbury in Wiltshire

City that hosted the 2004 Olympic Games

Famous town in Mali, on the southern edge of the Sahara

Located in Arizona, became a National Park in 1919

Prefecture in Japan, struck by an earthquake in March 2011

Site of a famous battle and title of an Abba song

EUROPEAN CENTRAL BANK 3

STONEHENGE 70

ATHENS 20

TIMBUKTU 2

THE GRAND CANYON 18

FUKUSHIMA 4

WATERLOO 75

INFLUENTIAL PLACES IN HISTORY

Stands on Bennelong Point in Sydney Harbour

The capital city of the Republic of Ireland

The largest public park in Manhattan

The northern end of the Earth's axis

The only surviving Wonder of the Ancient World

The world's largest coral-reef system

The world's most visited museum of 2011

SYDNEY OPERA HOUSE   61

DUBLIN   86

CENTRAL PARK   61

THE NORTH POLE   34

THE GREAT PYRAMID AND SPHINX OF GIZA   45

THE GREAT BARRIER REEF   43

THE LOUVRE   9

13
JESUS

Aha, Jesus: probably the most significant punctuation mark in the early history of our civilisation. Before Jesus, and the ordered life of the Roman Empire into which he was born, our history swirls around in a chaotic ungrammatical mess; a soup made up of legend, oral history, well-documented fact and arrant nonsense, with a few alphabetti spaghetti thrown in to zhuzh up the quiet bits. But then, from the birth of Jesus on, we not only get a new calendar, conveniently zeroed on New Year's Day precisely a week after Jesus' birth (time of birth: past 3 o'clock on a cold and frosty morning – shouldn't be too hard to pin down in Bethlehem's meteorological archives), but also a more literal account of what was going on courtesy of the New Testament (although it, too, isn't above throwing in the odd spaghettum in the interests of keeping the story rollicking along).

The significance of Jesus himself, though, was not just the radical message he was sending out (and it was radical:

he was all about redemption, forgiveness and equality: a tough sell in those days . . .) but the potent combination of that and the precise moment in our civilisation's history at which he appeared. A bit like with the emergence of the wheel, early philosophy or The Beatles, you can't help wondering if nature doesn't just seize upon certain things or people because of the huge evolutionary role they have to fulfil.

Christianity started out as a Judaic sect in the first century, but then quickly spread across Europe, and to Syria, Mesopotamia (those guys again!), Asia Minor, Egypt, Ethiopia and India, before becoming the state religion of the Roman Empire following Emperor Constantine's conversion to Christianity in the fourth century AD.

Arguably, if it hadn't been Christianity, some other religion, possibly Mithraism (a curious Roman 'mystery' cult which shares some key tenets with Christianity), would have taken up the strain and become the mainstream religion in Europe for two thousand years, but it *was* Christianity. Which means that Jesus, a man who lived only into his thirties at the beginning of the first millennium, before Facebook, *The Voice* or even the printing press, and with not much more than a pair of sandals and twelve friends to his name, became someone who managed to spread a message further, and whose name has been more exalted, more widely renowned, and for longer, than any other human being. So far.

Please name any of the people depicted in Leonardo da Vinci's painting 'The Last Supper'. Where more than one person has the same first name we are counting it only once.

ANDREW	7
BARTHOLOMEW	4
JAMES	16
JESUS	80
JOHN	59
JUDAS ISCARIOT	55
JUDE	6
MATTHEW	47
PETER	50
PHILIP	4
SIMON	13
THOMAS	22

JOKES

The most important development in human history – more than writing, more than fire, more than Monster Munch – is the invention of jokes. Before we had jokes, most conversations went like this.

'Knock knock.'
'Who's there?'
'Ugg.'
'How did you manage to knock, Ugg? I live in a cave, and the entrances to caves are typically covered in reeds or rushes.'

This conversation happened *every single day*, for around 98,000 years, but, luckily, jokes were on their way. There seems to be some academic agreement as to the oldest joke ever written. Unsurprisingly, it came from our old friends in Mesopotamia and was written around 1900 BC. It goes like this:

> 'Good evening "Live at the Apollo"! Is there anyone in from the Euphrates? What is it with people from the Tigris and how they irrigate their land? Okay, okay, here we go with my first joke, in fact *the first joke ever*:
>
> 'Something which has never occurred, a woman did not fart in her husband's lap.'

Lots to enjoy in this particular gag, mainly that it is about farting, which remains funny to this day. Also the Mesopotamian diet was notoriously rich in pulses. So not a terrible start to the entire history of comedy, and it is definitely funnier than the second joke ever written, which dates from around 300 years later. It begins:

> 'How do you entertain a bored Pharaoh?'

Perfectly good set-up for a gag here. And to give the Egyptians their due the punchline was not 'ask his Mummy' or 'Get Cleopatra to fart in his lap'. Unfortunately the punchline was:

> 'You sail a boatload of young women dressed only in fishing nets down the Nile and urge the Pharaoh to go catch a fish.'

I was fairly sure that the Bible had no jokes, but according to Professor Francesca Stavrakopoulou at the University of

Exeter, I am very wrong. Her finest example of biblical humour is the moment when a group of children tease the prophet Elisha for being bald and in his impotent fury he summons wild bears from the forest to maul and kill them. I'm going to say that, at best then, the Bible contains some slightly dark jokes.

So, jokes had very unstable beginnings, but things slowly improved. The first surviving joke book is the Roman *Philogelos* ('Laughter Lover'), including such gems as 'A miser writes a will and names himself as the heir', which these days is a perfectly normal Panama-based tax scheme.

The first recorded British joke, from the tenth century, was:

'What hangs at a man's thigh and wants to poke the hole that it's often poked before?'
'A key.'

After this came Shakespeare, then, twenty years later, *Last of the Summer Wine* and a glorious history of wonderful jokes, countless laughs, boundless joy and broad, broad smiles.

And all of this has of course led us to the greatly more sophisticated humour of the present day, where, for example, we very happily laugh along to YouTube videos of husbands farting on their wives' laps. *Plus ça change.*

SITCOM COUPLES

We are going to give you the character names of fourteen couples who have appeared in British sitcoms over the past fifty years. We'd like you to tell us the title of the show in which they famously appear, and work out which is the most obscure.

Adam Smallbone and Alex Smallbone

Basil Fawlty and Sybil Fawlty

Ben Harper and Susan Harper

Beverly Lincoln and Sean Lincoln

Frank Spencer and Betty Spencer

Hyacinth Bucket and Richard Bucket

Mark Corrigan and Sophie Chapman

REV   2

FAWLTY TOWERS   100

MY FAMILY   50

EPISODES   1

SOME MOTHERS DO 'AVE 'EM   64

KEEPING UP APPEARANCES   55

PEEP SHOW   5

SITCOM COUPLES

René Artois and Edith Artois

Ria Parkinson and Leonard Dunn

Rodney Trotter and Cassandra Trotter

Sergeant Wilson and Mrs Pike

Tim Canterbury and Dawn Tinsley

Victor Meldrew and Margaret Meldrew

Vince Pinner and Penny Warrender

'ALLO 'ALLO!   67

BUTTERFLIES   24

ONLY FOOLS AND HORSES   94

DAD'S ARMY   82

THE OFFICE   6

ONE FOOT IN THE GRAVE   76

JUST GOOD FRIENDS   18

15
THE FALL OF THE ROMAN EMPIRE

How on earth did they let this happen? How possibly could the most successful conquering and system-building force the world has so far seen (not to mention natty fashioners of leather and beadwork and ace road-builders) crumble to dust?

The Romans had it all: Italy, France, Germany, Spain, an awful lot of Britain, Turkey, bits of North Africa. The Panini sticker book of Roman Colonies ran to several volumes. There were so many places for Romans to go on holiday where everyone spoke Latin, wore togas, liked the same food and generally didn't want to kill them, it's amazing they got any work done at all.

And perhaps that was the problem. Perhaps, in fact, rather than being a surprise that it all fell to bits, it's more a miracle that the empire kept going for as long as it did. At its largest, the Roman Empire sprawled over a vast area comprising one-fifth of the whole world's population and covering a huge welter of different languages, cultures, ethnicities and world darts governing bodies: keeping up with all the paperwork and discipline – and, one has to remember, with only the most basic dial-up modems – was simply too much. By AD 117 they had reached the point where the citizens of the Roman Empire even outnumbered members of So Solid Crew.

If you wanted to start pointing fingers (and hey, who doesn't?) you could specifically blame the Goths for Rome's downfall. The Goths were a mass of peoples who crossed the Danube into the empire as refugees in the late fourth century. They were treated pretty shabbily by the Romans and so, utterly fed up, led a rebellion culminating in the Battle of Adrianople in 378.

Rome was aware of the Goths, indeed it had seen them sitting around in their long dark clothing at Roman bus stops, but had generally written them off as feckless adolescents with a worrying taste for the over-emotional and supermarket own-brand cider. This was to prove a fatal underestimation. They turned out to be pretty handy in a fight. At Adrianople vast numbers of them, more than the Roman generals had ever planned for, sauntered over the ridge, armed with heavy jewellery and painted in terrifying eyeliner, shouting slogans such as 'Give me the RING!!' and *'Bella Legosi mortem est!'* The Romans took the worst and most humiliating defeat of the empire's history. The Goths swiftly infiltrated and, after a brief party around a bonfire, pretty much took control of the Roman army. The empire, as it was, never recovered.

FIGURES OF THE ROMAN EMPIRE

We are going to give you twelve clues to characters from or connected to the Roman Empire. Can you work out who they are?

Derek Jacobi played him in the BBC classic 1976 TV series

Emperor who built a Palace in Split, Croatia

Emperor who gave his name to a line of fortifications across northern England

Emperor who was said to have fiddled while Rome burned

Gladiator who led slave revolt in 73 BC

He crossed the Alps with his army supported by elephants

He promised to appoint his horse to the Senate

He wrote the epic poem The Aeneid

His 30-metre-high marble column stands in Rome

Orator who wrote The Catiline Orations

Poet famous for his sixteen surviving Satires

Summarised his Asia Minor campaign as 'veni, vidi, vici'

CLAUDIUS	25
DIOCLETIAN	1
HADRIAN	56
NERO	55
SPARTACUS	24
HANNIBAL	49
CALIGULA	20
VIRGIL	9
TRAJAN	6
CICERO	7
JUVENAL	3
JULIUS CAESAR	28

16
ANGLO-SAXONS, VIKINGS, WOULD EVERYBODY PLEASE STOP INVADING?

As soon as the Romans left Britain in the fifth century the country became Northern Europe's convenient deserted holiday cottage; the one that gets burgled and singed and used for illegal parties and fights every weekend. A succession of rowdy mobs turned up, surveyed the place with their torches held high, saying 'oi, oi', and generally kicking the skirting boards. First it was the Picts from Scotland, who had been longing, ever since Hadrian had built his wall, to come over and razz it up down south. Then came the Scots – or Scoti – from (confusingly) Ireland, who were itching to have a good old pile-on with the Picts and the Britons. Then the Saxons turned up, from what is now the Danish/German border, presumably with a party keg or two, with their friends, the Angles (also from the Danish/German border – in fact identical in pretty much every way to the Saxons), and *their* friends the Jutes (who came from Jutland – a peninsula that prongs rather suggestively up between the pendulous landmasses of Sweden and Norway – which is also not a million miles away from the Danish/German border). Why all these peoples from the same corner of the Danish/German border had to have so many different names I don't know, but in they came, each with their own customs and (I'm guessing) their own brands of lager, and each adding some new note of cosmopolitan sophistication to what would gradually become the Anglo-Saxons: the People of Britain. In fact from 'Angle' comes the name 'England', so this could truly be looked upon as the time when our nation of once-disparate tribes was starting to come together.

Shortly afterwards, the Vikings arrived (late on in the eighth century), looking for some fun. Bafflingly, their first landing on these shores was in Dorset, which was the result either of impressive reconnaissance or simply of a burning need to visit Monkey World. On docking, they picked up their skirts, charged inland shouting 'BUNDLE!' and generally got stuck into the party, daubing some yeasty messages of their own onto the wall of our nation's bungalow.

Sometime during the eighth century, Denmark got it together and became a sovereign state (although one that preceded the UN by some 1,200 years, so it would have to wait a while before being recognised by that august body), weaving in a trice all the raggle-taggle strands of southern

Vikings, Jutes, Saxons, Gillans, Motorheads, and Black Sabbaths into one respectable cord of nationhood. And over in England the new Danish nation tussled like mad with its erstwhile countrymen for the English crown. This tussle went on right up to the Norman invasion on account of the strange and complex Danish/German-border-related allegiances that ran the length and breadth of the country. Initially the Anglo-Saxons held sway for a century or so (notably under King Alfred) but then things started to go the Danish way under their powerful King Harald Bluetooth. Indeed Sweyn, son of Bluetooth (Bluetooth 2.0), even took the English crown in 1013 but the Bluetooth line (despite its excellent – and wireless – connections) was to be short-lived because, as we all know, everything changed – in a meaningful and permanent way – on 28 September 1066.

Before the Norman Conquest the people of England were called things like Tostig, Stigant, Aegfrith and Cnut and were governed by a council called 'The Witan'. Afterwards they were called things like Jeremy and William and were governed by their insatiable need for a decent mid-price rosé.

FAMOUS NORDIC PEOPLE

We are going to give you fourteen clues to famous Nordic People. Can you work out who they are?

For the purpose of this question we are defining 'Nordic People' as those born in Sweden, Norway, Denmark and Finland.

A peace prize is named after this inventor of dynamite

A widely used temperature scale is named after him

Author of 1890 play *Hedda Gabler*

Composer of the tone poem 'Finlandia'

Directed the film *The Seventh Seal*

Fascist leader whose name has become a byword for traitor

His painting 'The Scream' was stolen in 2004

ALFRED NOBEL 53

ANDERS CELSIUS 10

HENRIK IBSEN 10

JEAN SIBELIUS 9

INGMAR BERGMAN 10

VIDKUN QUISLING 17

EDVARD MUNCH 24

FAMOUS NORDIC PEOPLE

Lead singer of A-Ha

Leader of the first expedition to reach the South Pole

Liverpool midfielder 1984 to 1996

She was a team captain on *Shooting Stars*

Won five consecutive men's singles titles at Wimbledon (1976–80)

Won the F1 Drivers' Championship in 1998 and 1999

Wrote the fairy story 'The Emperor's New Clothes'

MORTEN HARKET	25
ROALD AMUNDSEN	29
JAN MOLBY	4
ULRIKA JONSSON	36
BJORN BORG	45
MIKA HAKKINEN	6
HANS CHRISTIAN ANDERSEN	41

17
LONDON

No-one knows exactly where the name 'London' came from. Some say it is named after an ancient King Lud, others that it comes from the Celtic 'Lowonidonjon', meaning 'river too wide to ford', and I think it comes from the fact that the 'London Dungeon' and 'London Aquarium' were based there. I mean, that just makes sense, because no-one had to change the signs or so on.

What we do know is that the Romans established Londinium in AD 43. Just eighteen years later it was burnt to the ground by Queen Boudica and her Iceni tribe. They had only come to London to visit Madame Tussauds, but started drinking heavily on the train down from Norwich.

The Romans rebuilt Londinium stronger and more fire-proofy, and it quickly became the capital of Britannia. By the second century it had 60,000 inhabitants, many of them Cockneys, and it was even bigger than Colchester which, at the time, was impressive.

The Romans abandoned Londinium in the fifth century after their landlord put the rent up. They didn't even get their deposit back because they left burn marks on one of the sofas. The Anglo-Saxons very quickly took it over and renamed it Lundenwic, one of many rebrandings of London over the years. For a brief time in the seventh century it was called 'Snickers'.

By the eleventh century, London – or, as it was known at the time, 'Starburst' – was far and away the largest town in Britain, and has remained so ever since. Sometimes people complain when we do questions about the London tube map on *Pointless* because 'not everybody lives there', but they don't complain when we ask questions about capital cities of South American countries, so something doesn't add up. Unless a lot of our viewers live in Uruguay and I just didn't realise.

Elstree Studios, where we film *Pointless*, is quite near London, though no-one knows exactly where it is. Leading scientists believe it is near Hatfield, and those same scientists are now wrestling with the thorny question of where Hatfield is.

Lots of the things that happened in London from the eleventh century onwards will be covered in the rest of this book, including the Peasants' Revolt, the Black Death, the Great Fire of London, the emergence of Shakespeare, and Fulham beating Juventus 4–1 at Craven Cottage.

It has remained at the forefront of British political and commercial power ever since this time and has become deeply embedded in the cultural history of the United Kingdom, celebrated in countless works of literature and song, the most famous of which is this.

> London Bridge is falling down,
> Falling down, falling down.
> London Bridge is falling down,
> Health & Safety.

TIME ZONE

We are looking for the name of any country whose capital city reaches midnight on 31 December ahead of London in the UK.

As ever, by 'country' we mean any sovereign state which is a member of the UN in its own right.

And remember we are looking for the name of the COUNTRY not the capital city.

(Please note ISRAEL is not on this list as its capital city is disputed.)

AFGHANISTAN	4	CENTRAL AFRICAN REPUBLIC	3
ALBANIA	1	CHAD	0
ALGERIA	1	CHINA	42
ANDORRA	0	COMOROS	0
ANGOLA	0	CONGO	1
ARMENIA	2	CROATIA	3
AUSTRALIA	61	CYPRUS	9
AUSTRIA	3	CZECH REPUBLIC	5
AZERBAIJAN	2	DENMARK	9
BAHRAIN	0	DJIBOUTI	1
BANGLADESH	4	DRC	0
BELARUS	3	EGYPT	6
BELGIUM	3	EQUATORIAL GUINEA	0
BENIN	0	ERITREA	0
BHUTAN	1	ESTONIA	6
BOSNIA AND HERZEGOVINA	4	ETHIOPIA	0
BOTSWANA	0	FIJI	7
BRUNEI DARUSSALAM	2	FINLAND	5
BULGARIA	2	FRANCE	22
BURUNDI	0	GABON	0
CAMBODIA	5	GEORGIA	4
CAMEROON	0	GERMANY	23
		GREECE	8

HUNGARY	7	MALAYSIA	9
INDIA	25	MALDIVES	2
INDONESIA	4	MALTA	3
IRAN	9	MARSHALL ISLANDS	1
IRAQ	7	MAURITIUS	0
ITALY	15	MICRONESIA	0
JAPAN	33	MOLDOVA	1
JORDAN	1	MONACO	0
KAZAKHSTAN	6	MONGOLIA	5
KENYA	2	MONTENEGRO	1
KIRIBATI	2	MOZAMBIQUE	0
KUWAIT	0	MYANMAR	1
KYRGYZSTAN	2	NAMIBIA	0
LAOS	3	NAURU	0
LATVIA	4	NEPAL	2
LEBANON	1	NETHERLANDS	5
LESOTHO	0	NEW ZEALAND	44
LIBYA	3	NIGER	0
LIECHTENSTEIN	0	NIGERIA	1
LITHUANIA	3	NORTH KOREA	9
LUXEMBOURG	2	NORWAY	10
MACEDONIA	1	OMAN	1
MADAGASCAR	1	PAKISTAN	16
MALAWI	0	PALAU	0

PAPUA NEW GUINEA	3	SWAZILAND	0
PHILIPPINES	6	SWEDEN	14
POLAND	11	SWITZERLAND	9
QATAR	1	SYRIAN ARAB REPUBLIC	3
REPUBLIC OF KOREA	7	TAJIKISTAN	3
ROMANIA	1	TANZANIA	1
RUSSIA	30	THAILAND	27
RWANDA	0	TIMOR-LESTE	0
SAMOA	4	TONGA	4
SAN MARINO	0	TUNISIA	0
SAUDI ARABIA	4	TURKEY	16
SERBIA	2	TURKMENISTAN	4
SEYCHELLES	1	TUVALU	2
SINGAPORE	10	UGANDA	0
SLOVAKIA	3	UKRAINE	5
SLOVENIA	2	UNITED ARAB EMIRATES	0
SOLOMON ISLANDS	0	UZBEKISTAN	4
SOMALIA	0	VANUATU	2
SOUTH AFRICA	8	VIET NAM	6
SOUTH SUDAN	0	YEMEN	2
SPAIN	13	ZAMBIA	0
SRI LANKA	7	ZIMBABWE	0
SUDAN	1		

18
MEANWHILE, IN SCOTLAND

The northernmost part of Britain (as yet unnamed of course) had a very similar post-Roman knees-up to the one further south, only with the added fun of Norwegians in the mix. (In you come, Ásgeir, pop your furs on the bed upstairs, help yourself to mead!) Norway, doubtless inspired by Denmark, had started the journey towards nationhood in the eighth century (not in fact through a process of amicable settlement but one of who had the biggest horns on their helmets and who was better at doing the killing) and on discovering that their new country was a pretty poor specimen agriculturally speaking, they decided to make full use of its excellent sailing facilities and head over to the lands to the south to see if they were any better.

That bit of land nearest to them (the bit we today call Scotland) was by now turning into quite a mustering point for various discontented tribes looking for power and territory. At one stage the Roman Empire had stretched up to the Antonine Wall, which had run from the Firth of Clyde in the west to the Firth of Forth in the east. But this rampart was kind of more an ambition than a border (a bit like moving your fence halfway across your neighbour's garden late one night) and was overrun almost immediately after its completion in AD 154. It did, however, usefully mark the beginnings of Caledonia, a kingdom that stretched up to the north and was peopled by Picts. The Romans had come up with the name 'Picti' (meaning *painted ones*) on account – one assumes – of the warpaint they daubed themselves in rather than the frequency with which carefree Roman watercolourists would set up an easel to capture the noble beauty of these free-roaming guerrillas. To the west and out to the Western Isles, was the kingdom of Dál Riata (which, by the way, sounds *delicious*) where Gaelic-speaking Scoti people from Ireland had settled. To the south was the Brythonic kingdom of Strathclyde (peopled by Roman-influenced remnants of North Britain who roamed the lowlands moaning about the lack of decent olive oil and lute music, eventually settling happily in Morningside). When the Vikings (later trading as 'The Norwegians') first started landing and settling in the Shetlands and Orkneys and other parts of Caledonia, the Picts and the Gaels put aside their differences and joined up to see off the marauding Norsemen. It helped things along beautifully that both factions had recently started converting to Christianity so, despite their different languages, they presumably were able to bond and tell ribald jokes about vicars through the medium of sign language. This new nation of warlike rivals became known as Scotland and it was ruled over by the romantically named King Kenneth MacAlpin. King Kenny and his descendants ruled over Scotland with not a great deal of peace but certainly some stability for another two hundred years.

SCOTLAND

Here are some clues to facts about Scotland and its people. Can you give the answer you think the fewest of our 100 people knew?

1746 battle which saw the final defeat of the Jacobites under 'Bonnie Prince Charlie'

18th-century Scottish poet whose birthday is celebrated annually with a traditional supper

Author of the crime novel series featuring Inspector Rebus

City in which the devolved Scottish Parliament meets at Holyrood

City which contains the Govan district, known in the past for its shipbuilding

Former Scottish footballer who managed Liverpool FC for fifteen years from 1959

BATTLE OF CULLODEN   33

ROBERT BURNS   74

IAN RANKIN   22

EDINBURGH   69

GLASGOW   61

BILL SHANKLY   21

SCOTLAND

Islands to the north east of the mainland which form the northernmost point of the UK

Philosopher and economist featured on the Bank of England £20 note

Poet appointed as Makar, Scots national poet, in 2011

Politician who preceded Alex Salmond as First Minister of Scotland until 2007

Scottish band formed by identical twin brothers Charlie and Craig Reid

Scottish hero played by Mel Gibson in the 1995 film *Braveheart*

THE SHETLAND ISLANDS   42

ADAM SMITH   16

LIZ LOCHHEAD   2

JACK MCCONNELL   3

THE PROCLAIMERS   71

WILLIAM WALLACE   40

19
THE BATTLE OF HASTINGS

The Battle of Hastings was fought on 14 October 1066 between the essentially French Duke William II of Normandy and the Anglo-Saxon King Harold Godwinson. Godwinson is not a surname you see so much any more, which is actually kind of a spoiler alert as to what happened.

The climactic action took place around seven miles north of Hastings near the town of Battle, which, I'm going to say right now, is a place I would have avoided. In the same way, you should probably avoid visiting The Cape of No Return, or buying a death bed.

The English crown was at stake following the death of Edward the Confessor, or Edward the Grass as he was known in South London. Harold had already defeated two of his rivals, King Harald III of Norway, and his own brother Tostig at the Battle of Stamford Bridge, when William came ashore at Pevensey. Harold was forced to move his 7,000 troops down to the South Coast at speed. This was made all the harder due to rail engineering works at Haywards Heath, which meant there was a replacement bus service and no catering trolley.

The battle lasted from around 9 a.m. until dusk, much like a car-boot sale, and Harold's forces were defeated by the 10,000-strong Norman army. The climactic event was the death of Harold himself. The story that he died from an arrow through the eye does actually seem to be broadly true, though it is thought he was also attacked by a sword while he laid mortally wounded. This is all expertly depicted on the Bayeux Tapestry, an animated version of the entire battle voiced by Hugh Grant and Gérard Depardieu.

William was victorious, and he and his army celebrated with a game of conkers, and from there he got his nickname.

No-one is quite sure why the battle is called 'The Battle of Hastings', given that it occurred so far from Hastings itself. In the same way that no-one is quite sure why Ryanair say they're flying you to 'Rome'.

William marched northwards to claim the English crown, with a rag-tag assortment of remaining English leaders finally capitulating at Berkhamsted. Once again, leading scientists agree that Berkhamsted is somewhere near Elstree. No other information as to the whereabouts of Berkhamsted is available, though you will have landed at Berkhamsted airport if you have ever flown Ryanair to Edinburgh.

William was finally crowned in Westminster Abbey on Christmas Day 1066, which annoyed him in future years because Christmas and his coronation celebrations were on the same day and he always got joint presents.

It was famously revealed on *Who Do You Think You Are?* that Xander is directly descended from William the Conqueror. I often wonder what this King of England would have made of his family going up in the world like that.

WILLIAM THE CONQUEROR

We're going to give you five clues to facts about William the Conqueror. Can you deduce the answers?

Born in this modern-day country

Famous embroidered linen hanging depicting the Battle of Hastings

Hill on which Harold set his defence at the Battle of Hastings

Name of the great land survey commissioned by William

Year of the Battle of Hastings

FRANCE 24

BAYEUX TAPESTRY 50

SENLAC 2

DOMESDAY BOOK 14

1066 87

20
THE CRUSADES

Or, as I like to call it: How a Lot of Englishmen Went on a Very Bad Holiday By Mistake.

Picture the scene: you are a farmer in a muddy field on a cold Tuesday in the twilight of the eleventh century. A man comes galloping around your village in smart shiny armour with a trumpet, saying 'Let's go on an adventure! It'll be fun! We're going to retake Jerusalem from the barbarians! There might be some money in it! It'll definitely be sunny! Bring your SWIMMERS!!'

And so you do the only sane thing, which is to throw down your pitchfork, pack a few belongings in a kerchief and leave for the Middle East immediately.

This is absolutely more or less what happened up and down this country in 1095 after the Pope at the time, Urban II, responding to a plea from the Byzantine ruler Alexius, encouraged everyone who could lay their hands on so much as a sharp stick, to take back Jerusalem from the Muslims.

Religious fervour in late eleventh-century England was high and the response to this call to arms was tremendous. Some might say overwhelming. Some might say Urban II might have wondered what sort of a monster he had unleashed. I am picturing something very like the scene outside a Manchester conference centre on *X Factor* auditioning day.

An organised Crusade consisting of knights and proper soldiers set off, including tight bands of Templar Knights, who were to make their fortune during the Crusades lending money and building forts. But they were followed by a vast, shambling band of enthusiastic amateurs, armed to the teeth with bits of sharp wood, led by a popular preacher, Peter the Hermit (although how you can be a popular preacher while also fulfilling your calling as a hermit beats the hell out of me), and all hoping to make it to the Judges' Houses stage of the competition.

It turns out none of the Crusaders was entirely equipped for travel to far-off places. They didn't especially like the food in the picturesque cafés and bars of the Holy Land, couldn't get their heads around the local currency and weren't at all prepared for the sanitary arrangements. Hundreds died. Many hundreds more got sunburnt, like really badly sunburnt. Tracey from Renfrewshire, who belted out a memorable and poignant 'And I Am Telling You' to Urban II (joined by Sinitta), was sent home in a particularly emotional episode. And yet, somehow, four years later in 1099, this extraordinary ragbag Christian army did retake Jerusalem from the Muslims in a very undignified siege of the city that was bloodier than a *Game of Thrones* season finale (and with nearly as much nudity).

The Second Crusade was an embarrassing disaster, so let's skip over that and on to the next most famous Crusade, which was the Third Crusade in 1189. We know about this Crusade because it was led in part by our own King Richard I ('The Lionheart') of England.

Richard defeated Saladin – a key player in the area, who had retaken lands grabbed by the First Crusade – at the Battle of Arsuf in 1191. But Richard, short of supplies, fed up with a diet of olives, fish and haloumi, and unable to make it to Jerusalem with his army, did the next best thing, which was to sit down and negotiate a peace treaty with Saladin, which would allow unarmed Catholic pilgrims and traders to have safe passage into Jerusalem. Job – you might have thought – zagood'un.

There were more Crusades – loads more in fact (possibly as many as eight, possibly as many as a hundred, depending on how you measure these things) – but after Richard I disappeared from the scene (which he did straight after his sing-off with Saladin), British involvement rather tapered off as our fighting men generally had bigger fish to fry at home.

The Crusades dragged on into the fifteenth century as a sort of knightly sideline to our actual history (a bit like a series of *Gladiator* running at the same time as Wimbledon and the FIFA World Cup). A pursuit in which the bored youth of Europe could go off and hone their chivalrous skills in a kind of mindless Mike the Knight way, while also getting the chance to indulge in some top-notch suppression of other religions in a manner that remains a stain on our national character to this day. No-one came out of the episode especially well apart from Matthew Horton from Gillingham, whose version of 'Alleluia' was Number 1 in the Christmas chart in 1374.

ARTHURIAN LEGENDS

We are going to give you five clues to facts relating to the myths and legends concerning King Arthur. Can you work out the answers and pick the one that you think the fewest of our 100 people knew?

Author of 15th-century work *Morte D'Arthur*

Name of King Arthur's wife

Shape of the famous table Arthur sat at with his knights at court

Title of the 1963 animated Disney film about Arthur

Usual name of the sword given to Arthur by the Lady in the Lake

SIR THOMAS MALORY   9

GUINEVERE   49

ROUND   91

THE SWORD IN THE STONE   44

EXCALIBUR   69

21
THE DOMESDAY BOOK

The Domesday Book (published 1086) – A Review by
@BookEnjoyer1970

Was really looking forward to reading this. I had just finished the latest Ian Rankin (five stars) and was in the mood for a change of pace. I had heard a lot about the Domesday Book but it was one of those things I'd never read, so I thought why not?

Big mistake. I should have known better when I saw they'd spelt 'Doomsday' wrong, a mistake that Mr Stephen King (five stars) would not have made.

I don't know if you are an enormous fan of detailed catalogues of land and cattle ownership compiled for tax-gathering purposes by William the Conqueror, but I am not.

If you want to read a terrible book then this is for you. It's actually two terrible books, 'The Little Domesday Book' and 'The Great Domesday Book'.

I know what you're thinking: 'I'll read the little one.' Don't even bother, it's actually more complicated than the other one, even though it only covers Norfolk, Suffolk and Essex. And as for 'The *Great* Domesday Book', I don't think so!!!!!!! Apparently 'The Domesday Book' was enormously unpopular at the time, and I can see why.

The writer, Norman somebody, has such a clunky way with dialogue. Who even speaks in Medieval Latin these days? No-one, so it's boring.

So what if the whole of 'The Great Domesday Book' was transcribed by hand onto parchment by a single person? Buy a Mac, buddy. 'The Little Domesday Book' was written by six different people, and you can tell. It is literally all over the place.

There is a bit right at the beginning about a farmhouse and some pigs, and you think, 'Hold on, what's this, someone is going to steal a pig, and then there will be a trial and then the thief will fall in love with the daughter of the magistrate', but no, none of this happens. The pigs and the farmhouse are never mentioned again, but other farmhouses are, and other pigs too, and that is confusing. In all, it mentions 13,418 places. I'm supposed to remember that? At least *Game of Thrones* has dragons.

I simply don't get what all the hype is about. It just lists field after field after field and details tax paid and tax owed. In *The Girl on the Train* (five stars) our protagonist (no spoilers!) witnesses a murder, and the Domesday Book could really use something like this. Perhaps someone is driving past a field on a train (or a carriage, if they didn't have trains in 1086 – pedants) and sees a nobleman murdering a peasant, but the nobleman has a twin and they *both* confess but one *must* be lying! Imagine the fun Grisham (five stars) would have with this stuff! Or how about building a school for wizards on one of the smallholdings that the author seems determined to describe in tedious detail? Has the author really never heard of an alcoholic spy, or children finding a buried case full of money, or something about what would have happened if Hitler had won the war? It's not rocket science, Norman!!!!!!!

The reviews of this book are absurd. H. C. Darby, who described it as 'The most remarkable statistical document in the history of Europe', has clearly never read *Freakonomics* (five stars).

All this said, we did 'The Domesday Book' for book club and others enjoyed it.

(No stars)

EVENTS FROM HISTORY

Here is a list of twelve events from history. We would like you to tell us the centuries in which they occurred.

Remember, some of them may have occurred in the same century as other events on the list.

An English fleet defeated the 'Spanish Armada'

Napoleon exiled to Elba

Mark Zuckerberg co-founded Facebook

Charlemagne became king of the Franks

Domesday Survey undertaken

The Spinning Jenny was patented

16TH CENTURY (1588) 14

19TH CENTURY (1814) 18

21ST CENTURY (2004) 31

8TH CENTURY (768 AD) 1

11TH CENTURY (1086) 22

**18TH CENTURY (PATENTED BY
JAMES HARGREAVES 1770)** 15

EVENTS FROM HISTORY

St Patrick began his missionary work in Ireland

Samuel Pepys wrote his diary

Magna Carta signed

Queen Victoria married Prince Albert

Martin Luther published his *95 Theses*

Mussolini came to power in Italy

5TH CENTURY (IRISH ANNALS DATE HIS LANDING IN WICKLOW AS BEING IN 432 AD)   1

17TH CENTURY (1660-69)   18

13TH CENTURY (1215)   11

19TH CENTURY (1840)   43

16TH CENTURY (1517)   6

20TH CENTURY (1922)   39

22
BRUCE FORSYTH

'It's a BOY, Gamma Forsyth! A beautiful blue-eyed boy!' shrieked the girl, wiping her hands on the rough calico of her overalls as she ran out of the hut to tell the elders. Galadriel Brousilhandd St Croix Gordon Forsyth drew in his first breath and roared. The actual origins of Brousilhandd (or Brus as he came to be known) are lost in legend, with many different kingdoms claiming him as their own, but he would go on to be one of the most significant figures in Britain's folk history, his influence reaching right up to the north of Caledonia where he was revered as a 'hearth sprite', an ancient household deity responsible for familial cohesion and 'welefere in abune o' Saturne'en' (good cheer on Saturday evenings – a traditional weekly coming together for clans). In England, Brus (or Bruce – later Sirbruce) had a Sunday-night feast in his honour known as a Palladio, but there is some debate as to which of these, if any, was the official festival. Some historians even say both could be.

What is known (and documented) is that great dances were held in his honour every weekend from the nineteenth Sunday after Trinity to the Fourth Sunday of Advent, to which mummers, athletes and vassals would come to meet, partner – and frequently take on as amours – dancers from far-off kingdoms to the east. The old English expression 'forsooth' is a derivation of Forsyth and is attributed to Sirbruce.

BRUCE FORSYTH

We are looking for any UK TV show where Bruce Forsyth has been credited as either the host, compere or the presenter for at least ten episodes. We are not counting film roles or appearances in sitcoms.

BRUCE FORSYTH'S GENERATION GAME	48
BRUCE FORSYTH'S BIG NIGHT	0
BRUCE'S GUEST NIGHT	0
PRICE IS RIGHT	16
DIDN'T THEY DO WELL!	0
PLAY YOUR CARDS RIGHT	36
STRICTLY COME DANCING	46
SUNDAY NIGHT AT THE LONDON PALLADIUM	7
TAKEOVER BID	0
THE BRUCE FORSYTH SHOW	0
YOU BET!	1

23

THE MAGNA CARTA

The Magna Carta is one of the most important documents in British history, alongside the Act of Union and the lyrics to 'Baggy Trousers' by Madness. It has also had a huge impact on later documents such as the American Declaration of Independence and the European Convention on Human Rights. It is something of a big deal.

However it really only came into being as a way for King John to get out of trouble with a group of rebel barons who were demanding greater freedoms and lower taxes and threatening his rule. It clearly worked, as King John & The Rebel Barons later formed a formidable jazz sextet and successfully toured arts centres up and down the country.

The Magna Carta was signed at Runnymede, and it will surprise no keen readers of this book to discover that Runnymede is strongly believed to be somewhere near Elstree.

Successive monarchs modified the Magna Carta pretty

much at will, in the same way that we keep changing the endgame of *Pointless*. Whenever we do this some people get furious for about two weeks and then they worry about something else like dog passports or Fiona Bruce until next time we change it, and then they get furious again.

I'm assuming the same is true of the Magna Carta. It means, though, that of the sixty-three clauses contained in the original Magna Carta, sixty have since been rescinded. The three remaining clauses protect the rights and the liberties of the English Church (to overcharge for scones in their tearooms, for example), to protect the customs and rights of London and other major cities and ports, and, most famously of all, this:

No free man shall be taken or imprisoned, or be disseised of his freehold, or liberties, or free customs, or be outlawed, or exiled, or any other wise destroyed; nor will we not pass upon him, nor condemn him, but by lawful judgment of his peers, or by the law of the land. We will sell to no man, we will not deny or defer to any man either justice or right.

This is possibly the single most important sentence in the history of law and democracy, though, to this day, no-one has ever looked up what 'disseised' means. Suggs conspicuously avoided it in the lyrics to 'Baggy Trousers'.

So the Magna Carta today is almost unrecognisable from the original document, but still retains its awesome power. It's like if you ever go and see The Drifters in concert; none of the original members remain, but they'll still play 'Under the Boardwalk'.

It is not known how many copies of the original document were made, but just four remain. If you want to see one, and it is a genuinely moving experience, one is at Lincoln Cathedral, one at Salisbury Cathedral, one at the British Library and one in the downstairs loo at Xander's house.

It is also cool how it is spelt 'Carta' rather than 'Carter', as if it's a rapper.

THE MAGNA CARTA

Here are five clues to facts relating to the
Magna Carta. Can you give the answer that you
think the fewest of our 100 people knew?

Archbishop of Canterbury who was instrumental
in the sealing of the Magna Carta

King of England who accepted and sealed the Magna Carta

Number of clauses in the original document

US TV chat show host whose questions about it
stumped David Cameron

Year in which the Magna Carta was sealed

STEPHEN LANGTON 3

KING JOHN 38

63 0

DAVID LETTERMAN 35

1215 18

24
BLACK DEATH

You always get a hint, don't you, from the name of a disease, and it's not always a helpful one. Measles sounds appropriately unpleasant without being devastating. Shingles sounds like it might be rather invigorating. Mumps sounds like a hoot – Whooping Cough even more so. Black Death, by way of contrast, is one of those conditions that doesn't leave a lot open to interpretation.

Bubonic plague (Black Death's other name – in the same way Sting's other name is Gordon Sumner) has been around forever. It lurks in a dormant state for huge periods of time and then, when it feels its moment has come, the *Yersinia pestis* bacteria bursts out like a reformed boy band for a world tour. These tours very often start in the Far East, presumably because the merchandising opportunities are so spectacular, before sweeping across the globe.

The world had been very prosperous during Roman rule, with lots of sunshine and lovely holidays and great harvests, so everyone was fat and sunburnt and humanity was generally happy and healthy. But then in AD 536 the world was plunged into the Dark Ages. The clues seem to point towards a huge volcanic eruption taking place that year – studies of ice cores show deposits of sulphates which suggest a heavy blanket of volcanic fug in the atmosphere. By AD 540 trees had almost stopped growing and crops weren't doing too well either, so everyone who had been sitting out in the garden in 535, sandals swinging from their toes while they leafed through trivia tablets and sipped wine, was now starving. The sun had gone, Vitamin D pills hadn't been invented, and people were starting to get pale and snotty.

It was now that the little Louis Walsh of the bacteria world decided to get the band together. *Yersinia pestis* jumped onto a flea who jumped onto a black rat who jumped onto a boat that sailed to Egypt, and boom! The bubonic plague in its first incarnation ('Justinian's plague', after Eastern Roman Emperor Justinian I) took the world by storm. It killed up to 50 million people over a period of two hundred years and then it died out and went back into dormancy. By then the skies had cleared of volcanic debris and the Medieval Warm Period had arrived. Corks popped, sandals swung on toes again, and everyone got on with gathering in huge harvests, establishing countries and building cathedrals all over the place. Populations expanded and trade flourished from China all the way to Greenland, and Justinian's plague was forgotten.

Six hundred years later in the first half of the fourteenth

century, right in the middle of all this sunbathing and feasting and cavorting and building, the call came through from little Louis Walsh bacteria: it was time to put the band together again. Bubonic plague gets on its rat and off we go again. But this time it was considerably worse. The towns were much larger, sanitation was still very basic, and the flourishing trade links that had grown over the centuries meant that *Yersinia pestis* spread across Europe like wildfire. This time, hundreds of millions of people were killed by the plague – it's estimated that between 45 and 50 per cent of Europe's population was wiped out.

For those few still left standing though, it wasn't all bad. There were complaints from the rich that they couldn't find servants for love or money so by 1500 serfdom was dead too. The price of land went down as there was such a shortage of people to work it, and the lack of a reliable supply of workers encouraged the invention of machines, so you could say that the Industrial Revolution had its origins in the plague and its aftermath.

The plague came back for a somewhat quieter tour in the mid-nineteenth century but it was largely in arenas and town halls rather than the stadiums of the fourteenth century. The impact of this third plague was minimised in Europe by better sanitation. However, *Yersinia pestis* is still very much alive – a strain of bubonic plague emerged in Madagascar in 2014 that was resistant to drugs. Somewhere there's a little Irish bacillus looking at a calendar and making some calls.

MEDIEVAL ENGLAND

We are going to give you five clues to facts about the Medieval period in England. Do you know the answer to the most obscure?

Figure from folklore who robbed from the rich

First Norman King of England

French peasant girl nicknamed 'The Maid of Orleans'

Medieval poem that inspired the 2007 fantasy film with Ray Winstone

Year of the Battle of Hastings

ROBIN HOOD 89

WILLIAM THE CONQUEROR 37

JOAN OF ARC 52

BEOWULF 16

1066 95

25

THE PEASANTS' REVOLT

Anyone who has ever had to complain about anything will recognise what happened during the Peasants' Revolt. Here's a step-by-step guide to how one of the most famous social uprisings in British history was remarkably similar to that time you wanted Dawn from HR to provide free biscuits in the kitchen at work.

The basic grievances

THEM: Agricultural workers from Essex and Kent felt that some of their new-found freedoms were being curtailed by landowners, and also objected to having to work, free of charge, for the Church two days a week. The final straw came when a Poll Tax was imposed to help pay for yet another war with France.

YOU: When Mark was head of HR you had free biscuits. Now Dawn is saying that you can bring in your own biscuits, but the company will no longer provide them. Not even like, Rich Tea or something.

How it began

THEM: In 1381 a tax inspector visited Fobbing in Essex to investigate non-payment of taxes. The inspector was chased out of the village. Soon after, soldiers were sent to the village to restore order, but they were also chased out by armed locals. Emboldened, the good folk of Fobbing and other local villages began a march on London. The march picked up hundreds more disgruntled workers on the way, and workers in Kent began marching from the south. As numbers grew, so too did confidence, and this people's militia began to burn down tax offices en route to the capital.

YOU: You sent everyone an email asking why you should have to pay for your own biscuits and suggesting a meeting with Dawn to discuss. Probably on Monday because you work from home on Friday if you can.

Confrontation

THEM: The rebels were now led by Wat Tyler, who had somehow taken charge of the revolt, possibly in the same way that some poor unfortunate is forced to be Team Leader in the first week of *The Apprentice*. They met the fourteen-year-old King Richard II at Mile End and presented their demands. The young king, faced with such anger, immediately gave in to the demands.

YOU: You went to see Dawn on Monday and she said she would talk to management about the biscuits, but she was sure it wouldn't be a problem.

Other people causing trouble

THEM: Despite the success of the negotiations, the workers drunkenly began to run riot in London. They set fire to the countless official buildings, including the Savoy Palace and law offices in the Temple. They opened jails and hunted down and murdered immigrants, before marching on and capturing the Tower of London. In the Tower they murdered the Lord High Treasurer, Robert Hales, and Sudbury, the Archbishop of Canterbury. They paraded their heads through the streets before affixing them to spikes on London Bridge.

YOU: Michael in Accounts got wind of your meeting and sent everyone an email of his own saying that as he and others didn't eat the free biscuits (Michael is gluten-intolerant) he thought he deserved some other form of benefit such as a Nespresso machine or complimentary Shiatsu. You rolled your eyes, as this is textbook Michael.

The U-turn

THEM: Terrified by the violence of the previous day the Lord Mayor of London suggested that the king meet the rebels again, this time outside the city walls in Smithfield. At the meeting the king again agreed to all demands, but then the Lord Mayor killed Wat Tyler and the workers scattered back to Kent and Essex. Again, very similar to *The Apprentice*.

YOU: Dawn suggested a quick after-work drink in the Pitcher & Piano and told you that as Michael had put a cat among the pigeons, management had decided that free biscuits were probably more trouble than they were worth. You understood that her hands were tied and, after a quick gossip about Malcolm and Kerry (seriously, he's, what, fifteen years older than her?), you both went home.

The consequences

THEM: Government forces continued violently to quash more sparks of rebellion, in Essex, Kent and further afield, eventually murdering over one and a half thousand rebels. An uprising which began with simple, just and achievable aims had been brutally crushed, as would happen time and again in the future, as power desperately protected privilege.

YOU: You were a bit miffed. Michael didn't get what he wanted, but was happy because no-one else did either.

The moral

If we don't learn from history we are doomed to repeat it.

HORRIBLE HISTORIES FIGURES

We are going to give you five clues to famous historical figures, along with the year in which they died, who have been characterised performing songs on the children's TV series 'Horrible Histories'. We would like you to work out the answers and name the most obscure person.

Egyptian queen and lover of Julius Caesar and Mark Antony (30 BC)

English naturalist famous for his theory of evolution (1882)

Jamaican nurse who cared for British soldiers in the Crimean War (1881)

Queen of the Iceni people, destroyed the capital of Roman Britain (c. AD 60-1)

Scottish nationalist, led resistance forces against Edward I (1305)

CLEOPATRA   89

CHARLES DARWIN   72

MARY SEACOLE   9

BOUDICA   57

WILLIAM WALLACE   27

26
WALES

Wales is awesome, I think that is universally agreed. Quite apart from anything else, the Welsh are charming, funny and self-deprecating, and yet still manage to have a dragon on their flag. That is ballsy beyond belief. Finnish people are equally lovely, but they wouldn't dream of having a dragon on their flag.

If the history of Wales can be summed up, it is largely that the Welsh like to be left alone to enjoy themselves, people try to invade, the Welsh fight fiercely and eventually repel them, and then go back to enjoying themselves.

The Romans tried to invade and the Welsh just sort of settled in around them, took their money and waited for them to leave. The Angles and Saxons tried to invade and got short shrift. The Normans also had a pop and, for a while, were successful, until one morning the Welsh decided to have a good stretch, fetch their weapons and drive them back over the English border. England was, of course, an astonishingly easy country to invade, and was always far less cool about the whole thing than Wales.

The idea that England in some way conquered Wales is one of the most laughable ideas in British history. Edward I 'imposed his rule' on Wales after the death of Llywelyn ap Gruffydd. This was a rare error on the part of the Welsh. Llywelyn was also known as 'Llywelyn the Last', and you have to ask who on earth would choose a king with a name like that? It's simply asking for trouble. (See also 'Ethelred the Unready', 'Catherine the Doomed' and 'Olaf the Always Distracted By His Phone'.)

But if England was nominally in charge of Wales, then nobody told the Welsh. Henry VIII, for example, banned the use of the Welsh language in any official capacity in the mid-sixteenth century. In most normal countries (say Finland) this would lead to the slow death of the language, but here we are nearly six hundred years later and not only is Welsh still spoken, it is thriving. Nice try, Henry VIII.

Interestingly, earlier laws had banned any Welsh man from carrying arms or holding office, but also banned any English man who was married to a Welsh woman from the same. Which conveniently overlooks the fact that no man married to a Welsh woman could care less about carrying arms or holding office, because they have such an awesome wife.

So what if Wales officially became part of the kingdom of Great Britain in 1707, and part of the United Kingdom in 1801? It has carried on just the same. Through coal and steel, through non-conformist politics and non-conformist religion, through Dylan Thomas and the Manic Street Preachers, through being the straight-up nicest people you could meet who could drink you under the table and would walk you to your taxi, the Welsh humbly don't really care who imagines they're in charge; they just carry on happily being Welsh.

Big challenges face the Wales of today, from the collapse of traditional industries to what on earth to do with the 'man-bun' that Gareth Bale seems to be persisting with, but they face the challenges as always, with humour, with a calm knowledge of their superiority and with a great big dragon smack-bang in the middle of their flag.

WALES

Here is a list of fourteen singles by acts from Wales along with the year in which each song was a UK hit. Can you tell us the name of the artist or group who had the hit in the year shown?

All the groups on the list were formed in Wales, though the individual band members were not necessarily all born there.

CRAZY CHICK (2005)

GOLDFINGER (1964)

GREEN DOOR (1981)

HAVE A NICE DAY (2001)

I HEAR YOU KNOCKING (1970)

IF I RULED THE WORLD (1963)

IT'S A HEARTACHE (1977)

CHARLOTTE CHURCH   22

SHIRLEY BASSEY   77

SHAKIN' STEVENS   40

STEREOPHONICS   14

DAVE EDMUNDS   6

HARRY SECOMBE   19

BONNIE TYLER   28

WALES

IT'S NOT UNUSUAL (1965)

MERCY (2008)

ROAD RAGE (1998)

TELL LAURA I LOVE HER (1960)

THE MASSES AGAINST THE CLASSES (2000)

THOSE WERE THE DAYS (1968)

WALKING IN THE AIR (1985)

TOM JONES	89
DUFFY	30
CATATONIA	19
RICKY VALANCE	2
MANIC STREET PREACHERS	8
MARY HOPKIN	13
ALED JONES	48

27

THE PRINTING PRESS

The first ever press was a product of evolution. Of course it was, because you see the original press was the foot. No, no, no, bear with me here. A press is just any imprint that leaves extraordinary information (or sometimes wine . . .) behind it. And footprints – no, no, come back – footprints absolutely definitely do that. The Laetoli footprints in Tanzania, for example, date from the Plio-Pleistocene age and are the earliest proof archaeologists have that our very, very, very ancient ancestors used stone tools. They also show that man was bipedal from roughly 3.7 million years ago. A combination of the pattern of pressure in the footprint and the absence of any knuckle tracks dragging beautifully like musical staves on either side suggests that by this time we were walking in a leisurely fashion. A saunter, if you will. Imagine our ancestor now, proudly sauntering across the savannah to meet up with exciting new friends *from further away than they ever used to meet people when they just had to roll there* for a quick sun-downer and some Bombay mix and copious chat about *further away*. And there! That is the story told to us by this oldest of printing presses.

From there it was only a hop, skip and a jump (all right, a one-legged saunter, a double one-legged saunter and a double-footed saunter) to the next most famous imprint in history. In 1440, the German Johannes Gutenberg combined various existing technologies to create the printing press. The Gutenberg printing press used moveable typeface and could print many, many multiple copies of pages. It was put straight to use printing the Gutenberg Bible, various grammar textbooks and several thousand Tip Top Thai takeaway menus. So the story told to us by this printing press is one that is still going – and still delighting us – today: communication and education can be used for the advancement and benefit of all, along with the promise of chef's famous Jungle Curry delivered free to your door on orders over five florins.

The structure of society changed completely. Reading and learning spread across the middle classes of Europe and suddenly all you needed to build up a powerful following was a clear and well-reasoned argument or consistently good salt-and-pepper squid. A new age of political and philosophical engagement had arrived. Nothing would be the same again.

CHARLES DICKENS NOVELS

We are going to give you five sets of numbers that relate, in the style of a crossword clue, to the number of letters in the usual short titles of novels by Charles Dickens. We would like you to tell us the title of the novel that fits the numbers, and pick the one you think the fewest of our 100 people knew.

1,4,2,3,6

1,9,5

3,3,9,4

3,7,2,5,5

6,5

A TALE OF TWO CITIES   29

A CHRISTMAS CAROL   32

THE OLD CURIOSITY SHOP   16

THE MYSTERY OF EDWIN DROOD   2

OLIVER TWIST   40

28

HENRY VIII, ETC.

What everyone forgets about Henry VIII is that this great ton of venison in a man's clothes oversaw possibly the most important event in our social history. Stuff 1066, the date we should all remember is 1534 when Henry shut down the Catholic Church in our country, sacked the powerful monasteries and reclaimed all the massive wealth that was sloshing around for his people. Yes, he also had selfish reasons for breaking with the Catholic Church, and yes, the dramatis personae of who 'his people' were changed more often than the cast of *Neighbours*. But he oversaw a huge power shift of culture back to this country. He defended and re-established many more institutions than he destroyed. Our ancient universities, for example, and our cathedrals and their music schools saw a powerful surge in their output that was utterly astonishing and directly owing to the Reformation. Church music (dear to Henry's heart and therefore encouraged to prosper) flourished with a glut of Tudor composers, a purple patch that we will probably never see the like of again. England and then Great Britain rose through the rankings over the next hundred years from bit-part outsider to serious contender in the European league. Henry VIII was – in a great many ways – da man.

By the time he got round to divorcing Catherine of Aragon (his brother's wife, whom he married when he was seventeen) and marrying Anne Boleyn, he was getting on – in Medieval terms, he was an old man. He was forty-one! This was a man who, at the end of the day when he took off his padded shoulders and his exquisitely bejewelled doublet, must have liked nothing more than a good sit-down.

But still he hadn't had that son that he – and everyone else in the country – was anxious he should have. So you can see why he was getting a little bit itchy. If he didn't have a son, then Rome might once again exert its power and all that he had attained would have been for nothing. This is why he tossed aside wife after wife (a great many of whom – though not quite all – were called Catherine or Katherine). Just remember: Divorced, Beheaded, Died, Divorced, Beheaded, Went on to live in Gloucestershire (but not for very long).

Henry VIII above all else was a fiercely intelligent and cultured man – he was thought by many to be the finest and most charismatic ruler this country had ever had. He was, among other things, a poet and a composer of some repute (he wrote 'Greensleeves' after all). It was only in his latter years, as a result of brain damage caused by a jousting injury (so goes the modern thinking), that he became some-thing of a capricious lunatic, changing his mind ferociously every ten minutes about the smallest thing and expecting everyone to answer to the name Catherine or Katherine. But there was much more to his overall strategy than his own domestic comforts.

The Britain that we evolved into over the next few centu-ries would have been an infinitely poorer place had it not been for Henry VIII. It wouldn't have had 'Greensleeves', it wouldn't have had Thomas Tallis, we wouldn't have had our English enlightenment, and, most importantly, Trinity College, Cambridge would never have been founded, so 450 years later, Richard Osman and I would never have met, so perhaps Richard could have got to present *Pointless* with Sue Barker after all.

HENRY VIII

We are going to give you five clues to facts about King Henry VIII of England. Can you work out the most obscure answer?

His mother's name

The palace in which he was born

The title he was given by the Pope in 1521

The wife beside whom he is buried

The year in which he died

ELIZABETH OF YORK   10

GREENWICH PALACE   1

DEFENDER OF THE FAITH   17

JANE SEYMOUR   13

1547   6

29
SPANISH ARMADA

The Spanish Armada is probably one of the most famous armadas of all time. Name another armada? You can't. The Latvian Armada? You just made that up. The Renault Armada would be a good name for a car though.

The Armada was an attempt by King Philip II of Spain to invade England and wrest back control over the Spanish Netherlands. Quite how Spain was ever in control of the Netherlands I don't know; they certainly don't seem to vote for each other in Eurovision.

Anyway, despite being really famous, the absolute key to the Spanish Armada is that not much actually happened. If this comes up in your GCSE, you are laughing.

> A great big Armada one day set sail from Spain
> To try and make England Catholic again
> Philip sent his mighty battalions
> On frigates and cruisers and four mighty galleons

The ships were spotted by English patrols
While Francis Drake was still playing bowls
They anchored near Calais, a strange place to choose
To pick up more troops and some duty-free booze
Drake started thinking, somewhere near Dover
He set old ships alight and then sailed them straight over
The Spanish fleet panicked, it splintered and scattered
Formation in ruins and confidence shattered
The Armada retreated, invasion aborted
King Philip of Spain had been ruthlessly thwarted
No-one predicted how quick they would vanish
And that was the last that we saw of the Spanish.

And really that was pretty much it. There are other details, such as the Commander of the Spanish fleet, the Duke of Medina Sidonia, having never been to sea before, the Armada facing terrible storms as it was forced to flee via Scotland, and the Spanish fleet landing briefly in Ireland assuming they would be well treated and generally not killed, and being sorely mistaken in that assumption. However, these facts were harder to rhyme, so I've left them out.

The Spanish still call the Armada 'The Invincible Armada', and, while we may laugh, they have since managed to persuade us that paying £6 each for hundreds of tiny plates of food is a really good idea, so perhaps their plan was a different one all along.

FAMOUS SHIPWRECKS

We are going to give you five clues to facts about famous shipwrecks. Can you name the ships and work out which is the most obscure?

1997 film directed by James Cameron about this shipwreck

Collided with the liner *Stockholm* in 1956

Liner sunk by German U-boat south of Ireland in May 1915

Named for Henry VIII's sister and sank in 1545

Rescued 705 survivors from the famous 'unsinkable ship' in 1912

TITANIC	54
ANDREA DORIA	1
LUSITANIA	21
MARY ROSE	41
CARPATHIA	5

30
SHAKESPEARE

Poor old Shakespeare: being the nation's bard isn't all cakes and ale. Generations of schoolchildren have had Shakespeare thrown down in front of them and been told how wonderful he is. As any parent who has tried to teach their young children to share their enthusiasm for *University Challenge*, chicken jalfrezi or single malt whisky will know, these are often loves one is better off discovering for oneself. I once slightly oversold Victoria Sponge to my children, who all decided they hated it *before they'd even tried it*. Victoria Sponge, for goodness' sake! So yes, poor old Shakespeare – through no fault of his own, shunned by children. But it doesn't stop there for poor Bill . . .

I was once working with the writer of a much-loved sitcom series the very morning after the BBC had screened a special programme about Shakespeare and the great landmark of our culture that he had created. Strangely, though, this fabulous prime-time love-in hadn't been anything like as much fun for him as you might have hoped it would be. Why? Because throughout the ninety-minute programme, alongside all the funny clips from the series, were interviews with everyone involved, and every single person interviewed basically claimed to have written their bit of the show. So much so that – as my friend saw it – you could be forgiven for thinking that the writer was some sort of meek administrator who'd merely collated the shards of genius from the various actors it had been his good luck to fall in with. As a viewer I hadn't seen it quite like that, but ask anyone who has written something that's been successful (especially a comedy, strangely enough), and it seems to be a common theme. It must be the first sign of having written something truly timeless and special that everyone feels not only that it speaks to them but *from* them as well.

And this happened to Shakespeare too. This man of humble beginnings in sixteenth-century Warwickshire became not only the greatest, most admired and performed writer in the English language but also the greatest architect of the language too. His poetic phraseology has become everyday usage. Conversational English is lifting with coinages and words that he made up for us. But wouldn't you know it, his authorship is constantly contested. Not, admittedly, by the leading actors of his day (although you can bet that was only because The Globe Theatre didn't try to fill its schedules with cheap talking heads shows). But several theories abound about who 'Shakespeare' might have been. Some say he was just some impresario who published work by other talents, including Francis Bacon or Christopher Marlowe, in his own name; others think he was a pseudonym for the Earl of Oxford. The Oxford theory rests heavily on the fact that there are details in some of Shakespeare's plays that are strangely like details from Oxford's life, but hey, there's a lot in my life that closely resembles *Brideshead Revisited* but I am demonstrably not Evelyn Waugh. Also, twelve of Shakespeare's plays were written after Oxford's death, which for me clinches the argument. That and the fact that absolutely no proof has ever come to light of a link – however tenuous – between the two. The Oxfordians (as they're almost certainly not called) take this as further proof of Oxford's mastery of covering his tracks.

Shakespeare wrote 38 plays, 154 sonnets and countless other poems. He was balding on top, wore his hair long and had an earring. He married Anne Hathaway and is buried in Stratford-upon-Avon. Whoever wrote his plays – he was a genius one way or another.

SHAKESPEARE PLAYS

We are going to give you fourteen clues to the titles of plays by Shakespeare. Can you name the plays and work out which one the fewest of our 100 people knew?

A Capulet and a Montague fall in love

Achilles and Ulysses are characters in this play

Features the play within a play referred to as 'The Mousetrap'

Known as the 'Scottish Play'

Largely set in the Forest of Arden

Predominantly set in Berkshire

Shylock demands his pound of flesh

ROMEO AND JULIET	55
TROILUS AND CRESSIDA	0
HAMLET	2
MACBETH	75
AS YOU LIKE IT	0
THE MERRY WIVES OF WINDSOR	6
THE MERCHANT OF VENICE	35

SHAKESPEARE PLAYS

The character Falstaff first appears in this play

The History Play set most recently in time

The only one of his plays to have an animal in the title

The title character is father to Goneril, Regan and Cordelia

The title character is known as the 'Moor of Venice'

The title character is stabbed by Brutus

The title refers to the fifth of January

HENRY IV PART I   1

HENRY VIII   4

THE TAMING OF THE SHREW   12

KING LEAR   19

OTHELLO   21

JULIUS CAESAR   41

TWELFTH NIGHT   12

31

THE GUNPOWDER PLOT

We all feel we must surely know the story of the Gunpowder Plot, because Guy Fawkes remains so vivid and present in our national culture. But the truth behind the plot to murder King James (I of England, VI of Scotland) is truly extraordinary, and unbelievably gruesome and bloody. It resembles a seventeenth-century action movie, perhaps an early precursor to *Ocean's Thirteen*. Here is our gang . . .

ROBERT CATESBY – The Mastermind behind the operation. Six feet tall and handsome. Played by George Clooney.

THOMAS WINTOUR – The sidekick. A fine scholar and soldier. Played by Matt Damon wearing glasses.

JOHN WRIGHT – One of Europe's finest swordsmen. In those days, that actually meant he was good at using a sword, but, still, let's have Hugh Grant playing him.

GUY FAWKES – The explosives guy. Recruited by Wintour from the Spanish Netherlands, which until a couple of chapters ago I had never heard of, but which now seem to be everywhere. Fawkes will be played by Benedict Cumberbatch.

THOMAS PERCY – The next to be recruited was Percy, a sometime emissary to King James, who relied on his 'sword and personal courage'. He is played by Idris Elba.

CHRISTOPHER WRIGHT – John Wright's brother who had fought with Fawkes in the Spanish Netherlands – there it is again. As he is Hugh Grant's brother, Xander can play him.

ROBERT KEYES – 'A desperate man, ruined and indebted'. Looked after supplies. Played by Robert Downey Jr.

THOMAS BATES – Bates was Thomas Wintour's servant and only joined the plot after he discovered it accidentally. Given what eventually happened to him (no spoilers) he must be one of the unluckiest men in history. Played by Jack Black.

ROBERT WINTOUR AND JOHN GRANT – Thomas Wintour was, at this stage, recruiting pretty much anyone he found in his living room, and thus his brother and brother-in-law both joined the plot. We are getting a few too many characters now, so let's say that Robert Wintour can be the cool getaway driver and John Grant is the computer hacker guy. Played by Don Cheadle and Simon Pegg.

AMBROSE ROOKWOOD, SIR EVERARD DIGBY AND FRANCIS TRESHAM – They're just making these up now. Tom Hardy can play the first two and Kevin Spacey is Francis Tresham.

There are no women in this film because it is the seventeenth century.

The plot was to ignite thirty-six barrels of gunpowder under the House of Lords during the State Opening of Parliament on 5 November 1605 to promote the cause of English Catholics. The State Opening had been delayed a number of times due to the plague, and thus rumours of the plot had begun to leak out. An anonymous letter was sent to William Parker, 4th Baron Monteagle, warning that something was afoot, and the authorities were informed. No-one knows who wrote the letter, though it is possible it was sent by one of the conspirators' wives, so we may finally have a role for Uma Thurman.

King James ordered a search of the Palace of Westminster and Guy Fawkes was eventually discovered in the undercroft of a private house which extended under the Palace. Not only was he standing next to thirty-six barrels of gunpowder, he was also carrying matches. Imagine Cumberbatch's face when the cops ask him to turn out his pockets.

The plot was foiled, the conspirators fled in desperation, with the authorities in hot pursuit. So what happened to our little gang?

ROBERT CATESBY, THOMAS PERCY, JOHN WRIGHT AND CHRISTOPHER WRIGHT – All shot dead after a siege of Holbeche House somewhere near Elstree. The bodies of Catesby and Percy (Clooney and Elba) were later exhumed and their heads decapitated and displayed outside the House of Lords, like an ultra-hardcore Madame Tussauds.

SIR EVERARD DIGBY, ROBERT WINTOUR, JOHN GRANT AND THOMAS BATES – On 30 January they were dragged through the streets of London behind horses before being hanged, drawn and quartered. If you're uncertain what that means, it means they were hanged, then cut down while still conscious, their genitals were cut off and burnt in front of them and then they were disembowelled and fed to the crows. A bad day for Jack Black.

THOMAS WINTOUR, AMBROSE ROOKWOOD, ROBERT KEYES AND GUY FAWKES – The following day the same fate befell the next four conspirators. Of the four, one man managed to jump from the scaffold and break his neck before the agonies of mutilation. Who else but Guy Fawkes?

FRANCIS TRESHAM – There's a reason we cast Kevin Spacey as Francis Tresham. He was the only one of the plotters not to be executed, dying of natural causes instead. It is suspected that this is because it was Tresham who wrote the warning letter to the 4th Baron Monteagle, but, owing to a contract we have signed with Uma Thurman's agent, we are not going with that version.

JAMES I

We are going to give you five clues to facts about James I of England. Can you work out the answers and give the most obscure?

Century in which he became King of England

His regnal number as King of Scotland

Name of his Royal Dynasty

Name of his wife

Name of the European war that broke out fifteen years into his reign

17TH (THE 1600S)	24
VI	33
STUART	42
ANNE OF DENMARK	10
THIRTY YEARS' WAR	0

32
GALILEO

One look at the Leaning Tower of Pisa and it becomes immediately, wonderfully obvious how infallible mankind isn't. The tiny town of Pisa invested vast expense, time and energy into building something that would become famous for being *beautifully* wrong. In fact its exquisite and extravagantly built wrongness makes it poetic and adorable proof of what humanity can achieve while still being wholly misguided in its judgements. I like to think that Renaissance Italian brain-box and Pisa-dwelling questioner of received wisdoms Galileo Galilei drew the strength, from looking on that wonky campanile every day of his life, to question ever further the apparent certainties of seventeenth-century thinking. Maybe he didn't, maybe it was just the sheer boxiness of his brain that drove him on, but whatever the reason, he was forever pushing himself to think – as it were – outside that box. Inspired by Dutch experimentation with lenses, he went one step further and put two lenses together at either end of a long cylindrical pipe so he could peer into the heavens, further than anyone had ever peered before, quite possibly in the hope of finding intelligent lifeforms that could build towers that stood up straight.

Galileo did many other wonderful things besides appropriating intellectual property from nearby countries. He simultaneously dropped two cannon balls of different sizes from an identical height to show that they would hit the ground at the same time (to this day, this is one trick of Physics that I simply can't get my head around). Disappointingly – and I can't help thinking he missed a trick here – this experiment wasn't conducted from the top of the Leaning Tower (an event it was surely *made* for, but there you go – for all their pizzas and piazzas they've no pizzazz, these Pisa types).

Galileo was famously so bored during communion one day in 1581 that he used his pulse to time the swings of the bronze chandelier in Pisa's cathedral. Imagine being so bored of something that casual pew-physics begins to look like a diverting sideline! Anyhow, his observations led to his discovery that the time it takes for a pendulum to complete one swish is unaffected by the size of the swish's arc or the length of the string by which the pendulum swings (I *know*!). This led to the development of his idea for a pendulum clock.

Scientists tend to find fame once they find their catchphrase. Archimedes had 'Eureka!', Isaac Newton had 'Ouch!', Niels Bohr had 'What 'ave you done to me, Jeannie?' and

Galileo therefore also had to find one, so after much thought he went for, 'You're absolutely right, your Holiness, how stupid of me!' The Catholic Church, as it turns out (and boy did it turn out for him), rather had it in for poor Galileo. All of his discoveries had a way of contradicting the teachings of the Church. This led to him being questioned by the Spanish Inquisition, who found him guilty of heresy and sentenced him to death, unless he renounced his claims.

Galileo was nothing if not a pragmatist. Given the choice of burning at the stake or renouncing his so-called 'belief' that our solar system revolved around the sun, Galileo calmly and sensibly said he had got it all wrong. He spent the rest of his life under house arrest, looking up at the stars through his telescope, wondering where that straight tower might be . . .

ASTRONOMY

We are going to give you five clues to facts about Astronomy. Can you work out the answers? Those clues that are about planets refer to planets within the solar system.

2009 was the 40th anniversary of this famous landing

Name of the planet that is less dense than water

Name of the remnant of the supernova observed in AD 1054

The planet with the largest number of moons around it

The space telescope that was carried into orbit in 1990

FIRST MOON LANDING	78
SATURN	9
CRAB NEBULA	0
JUPITER	30
HUBBLE	42

33
THE GREAT FIRE OF LONDON

This entire book seems to have been just a series of people trying to set fire to London, so to be called 'The Great Fire of London' it must have been quite something. Let's look at some of the 'Great' things in history and see just how great they actually were. I will mark them all out of 10, which is what I believe proper historians like Tony Robinson do.

THE GREAT FIRE OF LONDON – Well, we've already seen that everyone from Boudica and the travelling Norwich City fans, to Wat Tyler with his *Apprentice* team 'Emancipated', and Benedict Cumberbatch, George Clooney and the rest of the gunpowder plotters, have all tried to set London ablaze without conspicuous success. 'The Great Fire of London', which was started in a branch of Greggs on Pudding Lane, destroyed 13,200 houses, 87 churches and St Paul's Cathedral.

It left 70,000 Londoners homeless, destroyed infrastructure and led to severe delays on the Victoria, Northern and Piccadilly lines. GREATNESS RATING: 7

THE GREAT WALL OF CHINA – It is a wall and it is, by some estimations, over 13,000 miles long, and it wasn't even built by five Polish guys. It was originally built because Mongolia's cat kept wandering into China's garden. So come on. GREATNESS RATING: 10

THE GREAT TRAIN ROBBERY – Stole around £50m in today's money, which is impressive because this was 1963, so to steal today's money somebody on the team must have invented some sort of time machine, which I think was a first. However, they almost all got caught, and the ones that didn't get caught can't be named for legal reasons (although one of them was *very* famous). GREATNESS RATING: 0

THE GREAT BARRIER REEF – We've covered this already, though I still can't believe it is alive. I mean, you wouldn't have coral as a pet. And if you did, what would you call it? I'd call it Carol I think. GREATNESS RATING: 10

THE GREAT LEAP FORWARD – Mao Zedong's attempt to turn the Chinese economy from agrarian to industrialised and collectivised between 1958 and 1961. One of the most disastrous, ill-conceived, violent and terrible episodes in human history, leading to over 18 million deaths. GREATNESS RATING: 0

GREAT WESTERN RAILWAY –If you've ever been delayed going to Bristol or Swansea, or sat in an overheated or freezing carriage somewhere outside Didcot unable to find somewhere to charge your phone, which has been rendered useless because their wi-fi is as jumpy as a meerkat expecting a package, you have Great Western Railway to thank. As is so often the case though, the staff are unfailingly lovely and therefore I am going to score it higher than the greatest mass killing in human history. GREATNESS RATING: 1

THE GREAT PYRAMID OF GIZA – The largest of the three pyramids at Giza, and the only one of the Seven Wonders of the Ancient World still largely intact. But it is right next to two other pyramids, so it's not *that* amazing. But it is over 400 feet high and inspired the Swiss to make Toblerone, so I am giving extra marks for that. GREATNESS RATING: 8

THE GREAT DEPRESSION – The feeling you get when you're travelling home from *Pointless* with your partner, who has just looked at a picture of British figure-skater John Curry in the head-to-head round and identified him as Bert Kwouk. GREATNESS RATING: 6

THE GREAT EXHIBITION – Held inside a mighty 'Crystal Palace' in Hyde Park in 1851. It was just an exhibition really. These days they hold 'Winter Wonderland' in Hyde Park, and that's much better. GREATNESS RATING: 3

THE GREAT BRITISH BAKE-OFF – Proof that we can now bake things without setting fire to the whole of London. Progress. GREATNESS RATING: 7

THE 17TH CENTURY

We are going to give you fourteen clues to facts about the 17th century. Can you give an answer for the most obscure fact?

'Of Man's First Disobedience' are the opening words to this epic poem by Milton

From 1675 this London Cathedral was rebuilt to designs by Sir Christopher Wren

Guy Fawkes and Robert Catesby attempted to blow up this building

In 1610 Galileo observed four moons revolving around this planet

In 1690 William of Orange defeated King James II on the banks of this Irish river

In 1692 nineteen 'witches' were executed as a result of the Witch Trials in this Massachusetts town

In 1698 Tsar Peter the Great imposed a tax on this facial feature

PARADISE LOST   12

ST PAUL'S   45

HOUSES OF PARLIAMENT   60

JUPITER   21

THE BOYNE   7

SALEM   44

BEARDS   28

THE 17TH CENTURY

James Stuart became England's first Stuart king but he was James VI of this country

John Lilburne was a leader of this group who demanded universal male suffrage in the 1640s

On 16 September 1620 a group of Puritans left from Plymouth for America on this ship

Poussin painted 'A Dance to the Music of _____' which is now in the Wallace Collection

The Great Fire of London started in 1666 in this lane

The Treaty of Westphalia in 1648 ended this conflict which was named after its length in years

This American University was founded near Boston in 1636

SCOTLAND	47
LEVELLERS	2
MAYFLOWER	36
TIME	4
PUDDING LANE	54
THIRTY YEARS' WAR	3
HARVARD	20

34

NEWTON'S CRADLE

Newton's   main
purpose   in life
was   to find out
how   to turn
lead into
       gold.
As a   hobby
he studied,   notoriously,
apples   falling from
     trees,

the   movements
of   the
planets   and
in passing   invented
calculus.   He
lived   in
fear   of

being   exposed

as

a

magic-

i-

an.

FAMOUS SCIENTISTS

Here is a list of famous scientists. Can you tell us which modern-day country they were born in?

To clarify, we are after the modern-day countries where their birthplaces are located.

ALBERT EINSTEIN

ALESSANDRO VOLTA

ALFRED NOBEL

ARISTOTLE

DENNIS GABOR

ERNEST RUTHERFORD

FRANCIS BEAUFORT

HIDEKI YUKAWA

LOUIS PASTEUR

MARIE CURIE

PIERRE CURIE

WILHELM RONTGEN

GERMANY	38
ITALY	20
SWEDEN	10
GREECE	60
HUNGARY	5
NEW ZEALAND	0
REPUBLIC OF IRELAND	1
JAPAN	37
FRANCE	66
POLAND	4
FRANCE	49
GERMANY	20

35

DR JOHNSON'S *A DICTIONARY OF THE ENGLISH LANGUAGE* (1755)

A
Brilliantly
Comprehensive*
Dictionary
Entirely
From
Great
Historical
Innovator
Johnson.†

* 42,773 words and around 114,000 literary quotations.
† Samuel Johnson has been described as 'arguably the most distinguished man of letters in English history'.

Key
Lexicographers[‡]
Mounted
No
Objections.[§]
Praised
Quickly,
Received
Stupendously,[¶]
Though
Ultimately
Very
Wordy.
(Xander
Yacht
Zebra)[**]

‡ Susie Dent.

§ Scholars were united in praise for this extraordinary achievement, which had taken Johnson over nine years to compile.

¶ The public also loved the dictionary. Johnson's biographer, Boswell, says 'the world contemplated with wonder so stupendous a work achieved by one man'.

** A botched climax. Doesn't ever feel great. Honestly, it justifies knowing lots more nouns or prepositions. Quite random, sorry, these utterly vacuous words. X-ray yak zoo.

WORDS ABOUT WORDS

We are going to give you a list of definitions of words that are themselves used to describe other types of words. In each case we've given you the word with alternate letters missing. As ever, we'd like you to identify the most obscure word.

Newly coined word
N_O_O_I_M

One of two words with similar meanings
S_N_N_M

Word formed from parts of other words
P_R_M_N_E_U

Word which is the same backwards as forwards
P_L_N_R_M_

Word which mimics the sound it describes
O_O_A_O_O_I_

NEOLOGISM   10

SYNONYM   81

PORTMANTEAU   8

PALINDROME   56

ONOMATOPOEIA   37

36

AMERICAN WAR OF INDEPENDENCE

Tax is always an emotive issue. In fact wherever you encounter social unrest, war, revolution or rebellion in history, you can bet anything you like that – whatever the underlying general unrest may be caused by – tax will have been the spark that kicked it all off.

As it (mostly) is here. In the mid-eighteenth century, the disparate states of America were motoring along, doing brilliantly – having come miles and miles since their humble and rather precarious beginnings in Jamestown and Plymouth back at the start of the 1600s where they were tilling the frozen earth with their bare hands and didn't know if they were going to survive the winter.

In fact, Americans really felt very American by the 1770s, and not really British at all, in the same way that we don't feel especially 'Victorian' now. And they were pretty fed up with having to pay the endless taxes that the British demanded from the tremendous success they were making of themselves.

The Americans protested and boycotted and grumbled along until 1773 when things came to a head when an anti-British faction called the Sons of Liberty (who I'm picturing in slightly baggy superhero costumes) tipped a consignment of tea into Boston Harbour.

It was a masterful PR stunt: tea, that most English and refined of commodities, was supplied by the East India Company and taxed to high heaven – the cost then being passed on to the average American consumer. Those boxes of tea represented everything that was wrong with British rule to the Sons4Liberty and in tipping it out they sent a very strong 'no more tea, vicar' message back to base. Plus 'The Boston Tea Party' is just the kind of event nickname that headline writers – then and now – live for, and once coined such names stay in the public imagination for centuries.

By 1776 the various states of America had got themselves together to vote for independence from Britain and signed the declaration on the 4th of July. General George Washington – at a wonderfully loose end around this time because there was no 'United States of America' yet for him to be president of – was appointed head of America's fighting forces and they and the British duked it out with musketry, tunics and gunpowder to decide what the best course of action should be. It's interesting to note that France and Spain also rallied to the Americans' side. France, because it was always hilarious to give the Brits a bloody nose, and Spain because they had some Sea Miles left that were about to expire and they fancied a laugh.

By 1782 the British knew they were beaten. France went away cackling, swigging from a flagon and wiping its mouth on its arm; Spain was given control of Florida (which is why Julio Iglesias still sells out the Sun Life Stadium in Miami); and the Americans were left in peace quietly to pursue their own course to power and world dominion.

AMERICAN PRESIDENTS

We are going to give you twelve clues which will lead you to the names of US Presidents. Can you work out the names of the Presidents and deduce which is the most obscure?

Appeared in over 50 Hollywood films before becoming President

Appears on the US Federal Reserve One Dollar bill currently in general circulation

Assassinated by John Wilkes Booth

Gave his name to a so-called 'Doctrine' of 1823 about US Foreign Policy

Initiated the New Deal program to alleviate the recession

Peanut farmer from Georgia

RONALD REAGAN 56

GEORGE WASHINGTON 19

ABRAHAM LINCOLN 44

JAMES MONROE 2

FRANKLIN D. ROOSEVELT 1

JIMMY CARTER 33

AMERICAN PRESIDENTS

President during the Cuban Missile Crisis

President during First World War

President on VJ Day at the end of Second World War

President who was born in Hawaii

Primary author of the Declaration of Independence before becoming President

The teddy bear is allegedly named after him

JOHN F. KENNEDY   29

WOODROW WILSON   6

HARRY S. TRUMAN   10

BARACK OBAMA   48

THOMAS JEFFERSON   1

THEODORE ROOSEVELT   70

37

THE INDUSTRIAL REVOLUTION

Now, full disclosure. Not only did I study the Industrial Revolution for O-Level, I also studied it for A-Level. This means I spent four years studying the causes of, the achievements of, the effects of, and the drawbacks of the Industrial Revolution, and I managed an A grade in both exams. Four years of reading, four years of lessons, four years of homework.

Here is what I am going to do. I am now going to write down EVERY SINGLE THING I remember about the Industrial Revolution from my extensive studies.

In doing so I hope to tell you a little about this extraordinary period of British history, almost unmatched in terms of the speed and scale of societal change. I also hope to tell you a little about the quality of comprehensive school education available in 1980s Britain. But mainly I hope to tell you about what a terrible fraud I am.

Here goes. I promise I will write down EVERYTHING I remember.

Something about the Enclosures Act, which was to do with fields, and which was connected, at a later date I think, to the Corn Laws and, much more importantly, to the repeal of the Corn Laws, which were something of a big deal. I want to say the date 1815 here.

Wool was tremendously important, as was cotton. The North West became a centre of the wool and cotton trade, because the weather is damp and that makes wool and cotton easier to work with. Or maybe just wool, but, either way, how do I remember that? There were lots of inventions, like the Spinning Jenny, which I'm going to say was Samuel Crompton, though immediately I say this I remember that Crompton invented Crompton's Mule, which was something different. Maybe it was 'Compton', but I'm fairly confident with 'Crompton'. I think the Spinning Jenny was James Hargreaves then. There was also Eli Whitney's 'Gin (short for 'engine'). Wool and cotton were a BIG DEAL.

Iron and steel were also a big deal. Iron was smelted, and there was something about 'pig iron' because of the shape of the foundries where it was smelted. Robert Owen had a foundry or smelting works in Wales, and there was something else important about him. Abraham Darby III built the world's first iron bridge, in Shropshire, and we had a picture of it on *Pointless* and I got it right.

Steam was a big deal, and led to a new generation of factory machines. James Naismith invented a steam hammer, Newcomen built a steam engine which pumped water from tin mines in Cornwall, and, of course, who can forget James Watt and the many, many things he did?

People moved from the countryside to the cities to work in the new factories. Conditions were grim beyond words, leading to the Factory Acts, which improved things a little. Smoke from chimneys turned silver birch trees black with soot, and all the white butterflies died out because they were no longer camouflaged from predators.

Then there were canals, of course. The Duke of Bridgewater was involved. Thomas Telford built roads and I think invented a different system of drainage. Isambard Kingdom Brunel was up to all sorts. I want to say John McAdam invented tarmac? I may have got that wrong. People sure were building roads though.

Okay, I think that has pretty much covered what I learned. I apologise if you are a history teacher, and I particularly apologise if you were my history teacher.

I haven't remembered a lot of the facts I was taught. I remembered them for as long as I needed to pass my exams and then they slipped away, shortly to be replaced by my encyclopaedic knowledge of the Stone Roses, World Snooker and The Films of Quentin Tarantino. I was lucky enough to slip into an industry, television, where this sort of knowledge is still held in pretty high regard.

But all this is my fault, not the fault of my teachers. And

what I have always kept with me, while the names and dates have crumbled to dust, is what the Industrial Revolution actually *meant*. What it gave us, in terms of the beauty of creative endeavour and progress, the extraordinary minds who conjured progress from nowhere and propelled Britain into an unimaginable future, bringing prosperity and opportunity in its wake. But also what it cost us, in terms of the dehumanisation of labour, of the gruesomely awful treatment of innocent people in the naked pursuit of capital and wealth for the few. It also taught me the fact that most of human history, most of what we call 'progress', lies somewhere in the grey depths between those two forces.

For that knowledge, which still informs me every day of my life, I thank my teachers. It turns out you knew what you were doing all along.

FICTIONAL COMPANIES

We're going to give you fifteen fictional companies from television series. We want you to tell us the television series in which these companies first appeared. As ever, we're after the most obscure answer.

BALDWIN'S CASUALS

EWING OIL

FENNER FASHIONS

GLOBELINK NEWS

HAMMOND TRANSPORT SERVICES

JUPITER MINING CORPORATION

MCKENZIE, BRACKMAN, CHANEY, KUZAK

PEARTREE PRODUCTIONS

CORONATION STREET   50

DALLAS   84

THE RAG TRADE   13

DROP THE DEAD DONKEY   9

THE BROTHERS   7

RED DWARF   9

LA LAW   3

I'M ALAN PARTRIDGE   3

FICTIONAL COMPANIES

SLATE ROCK AND GRAVEL COMPANY

SPACELY SPACE SPROCKETS

STERLING COOPER

THE BLUTH COMPANY

THE LUXTON & DISTRICT TRACTION COMPANY

TROTTERS INDEPENDENT TRADING

WERNHAM HOGG

THE FLINTSTONES   18

THE JETSONS   3

MAD MEN   7

ARRESTED DEVELOPMENT   4

ON THE BUSES   10

ONLY FOOLS AND HORSES   75

THE OFFICE   14

38

NAPOLEON

Napoleon's story is a sad one really. In a few short years he went from dominating Europe to miserable exile and death on a godforsaken island in the South Atlantic. The truth is that he was an excellent short-term battle-manager but a poor strategic thinker and his ultimate fate was the price he paid for his gambler's instincts and intellectual shortcomings. It is a curious fact that as a young man Napoleon had contemplated enlisting in the Royal Navy – we might now be remembering Nelson merely as one of Napoleon's captains at Trafalgar. On such apparently whimsical decisions does the fate of nations turn . . .

One of life's great opportunists, Napoleon took France from a delirious riot of egalitarian bloodlust, where the civic alternatives were equality or death, and turned it into a hereditary European empire blessed by the Pope, in which the thrones of Europe were handed out to his otherwise unremarkable relations while the Holy Roman Emperor admitted him to the bed of his daughter.

But none of this was well thought through. As Emperor, Napoleon had emblazoned on his battle flags 'Liberté, Egalité and Fraternité' but he still managed to establish the first police state in Europe (it was just his bad luck that the camera had not been invented, otherwise his identity cards would have been even more effective in controlling the population). It was terribly confusing to one and all – the French could never make up their minds if they were a republic or a monarchy. Nor were the other European states, monarchist or nationalist, ever sure where they stood. The Poles, even though Napoleon did nothing for them except to inspire their national anthem, remember him with affection; the Prussians, devastated by a French invasion, revenged themselves at least twice, in 1815 when they saved the British at Waterloo, and in 1870 when they destroyed his nephew and reduced France to a state of abject submission.

Napoleon also failed to comply with the fourth of Field Marshal Montgomery's rules of warfare. The first three were:

1. maintain morale by
2. winning,
3. and burying the dead as quickly as possible.

The fourth was 'never, in any circumstances whatsoever, march on Moscow'.

But at least he got a railway station named after his defeat at Waterloo.

BATTLE OF WATERLOO

We are going to give you five clues to facts about the Battle of Waterloo. Please work out the answers and pick which you think is the most obscure.

Commander of the British Troops

French Emperor who was defeated

Modern-day country in which the village of Waterloo is located

Said to have been won on the 'playing fields' of this school

Year in which it occurred

DUKE OF WELLINGTON   36

NAPOLEON I   81

BELGIUM   28

ETON   44

1815   23

39
STEPHENSON'S *ROCKET* AND THE RAINHILL TRIALS

Stephenson's *Rocket* was not the first steam locomotive, but it was the first to combine several key elements of steam engine design, and thus became the most successful and celebrated locomotive of its day.

The *Rocket* was designed by Robert Stephenson, with help from his dad, George. This essentially meant that Robert designed it while George popped in from time to time saying, 'Call that a steam engine? It's just a lot of noise', before asking Robert to stop hammering as he was trying to watch a *Top Gear* repeat on Dave.

The *Rocket*, and subsequent improvements made by the Stephensons, set the standard for steam locomotives for the next 100 years, and its pre-eminence began when it won the Rainhill Trials.

The Rainhill Trials were a competition set up by the

Liverpool and Manchester Railway in 1829 to find the best steam locomotive to run on its newly created line. Trains had to complete a series of runs along a flat, mile-long stretch of track near Rainhill in Lancashire. To make things harder, each train also had to carry a full film crew and Michael Portillo throughout the journey.

There was a massive prize of £500 – these days enough to buy an off-peak return from Euston to Manchester Piccadilly – and five engines were entered. Each was named exactly like a team from *The Apprentice*.

There was:

Perseverance ('Guys, I think it just says we never give up, we are united, and we would be good at buying leather hats in a Moroccan market.')

Novelty ('It says we have a sense of fun, sure, but that we're unique, and that we would be good at selling fish to commuters.')

Cycloped ('I just think it says, we looked at the word "encyclopaedia" then took some of the letters out, and we would be good at making an advert for gluten-free dog food.')

Sans Pareil ('It's French for "without equal" and it says we're the only team with someone who went to university and who thinks they are bound to win but will be kicked out in the first week because they are insufferable.')

Rocket ('It says, we're a firework, we're an ice lolly, we're

Ronnie O'Sullivan's nickname, and you can trust us to disastrously pitch a children's toy with very sharp edges to the Chief Executive of the Early Learning Centre with our flies undone.')

The first engine to drop out of the trials was *Cycloped*, which, for reasons best known to its creator, Thomas Brandreth, was powered by a horse, which proved too heavy and fell through the engine floor. You'll be delighted to hear that the horse was unharmed, although, as this was 188 years ago, it is no longer alive.

The next engine to drop out was, ironically, *Perseverance*. They really should have called it 'Yeah, Whatever'.

Third to go was *Novelty*, which was caught cheating by using a Rail Replacement Bus Service halfway through. It also had no wi-fi.

Sans Pareil very nearly beat the *Rocket*, proving fast and reliable, reaching speeds of up to 28mph, before disaster struck when a leaf fell on the line.

And so the *Rocket* was the only engine successfully to complete the trials and it went into service on the Liverpool and Manchester line the following year, famously hitting and killing the Liverpool MP William Huskisson on its very first day of service. It remains, to this day, the most famous steam locomotive of all time.

If you want to see the *Rocket* now, you can; it is housed at the Science Museum in London. Though good luck getting there on time.

EXPLORERS AND AVIATORS

These are all people who have found fame as explorers or pioneers in aviation or space. We will accept just the surnames.

Brothers achieving the first powered flight in 1903

Commanded the *Endeavour* in 1768

First Englishman to sail around the world

First European to cross the Pacific Ocean

First female to fly solo from UK to Australia

First man to visit both South and North Poles

First man to walk on the moon

First Solo Flight across the Atlantic

THE WRIGHT BROTHERS	73
CAPTAIN JAMES COOK	16
FRANCIS DRAKE	7
FERDINAND MAGELLAN	4
AMY JOHNSON	4
(SIR) RANULPH FIENNES	0
NEIL ARMSTRONG	67
CHARLES LINDBERGH	9

EXPLORERS AND AVIATORS

First to fly solo across the English Channel

First to reach the South Pole

First woman in space

First woman to fly alone across the Atlantic

He named 'Virginia' after Queen Elizabeth I

Led the *Endurance* expedition to the South Pole

North and South America named after him

LOUIS BLERIOT	9
ROALD AMUNDSEN	9
VALENTINA TERESHKOVA	6
AMELIA EARHART	19
WALTER RALEIGH	14
ERNEST SHACKLETON	4
AMERIGO VESPUCCI	8

ELECTRICITY

Ben Franklin did all right in life. Between inventing electricity and America, he has a pretty decent CV. I say invented, but really he *discovered* electricity. And he certainly didn't discover America. Although saying anyone *discovered* America is like saying you *discovered* a fantastic little bar in Shoreditch, or you *discovered* how to do italics on your computer. Tell it to the Vikings. Or the Amerindians down south. Anyhow. He came across – and became a pioneer in – the field of electricity. Because *electricity* was already a thing.

Electricity was probably first 'discovered' (certainly it was first named) by the English scientist William Gilbert in the early seventeenth century. Gilbert found that by rubbing amber, a static charge could be produced – in fact the word 'electricity' comes from the Greek word for amber ('elektron'). This makes me wonder just how many other activities (waltzing with magnesium, taking silver up west for a show and maybe a bite to eat, shouting at tin in French) Gilbert must have tried, and with what other substances, before getting somewhere with amber.

Luigi Galvani, an Italian in the late eighteenth century, made further interesting electrical discoveries. While working away one day during an electrical storm, Galvani found that the small static charge in his scalpel – caused by the atmospheric conditions – was enough to make the legs of a dead frog (I mean, how much time did these Italians have on their hands?) dance around. This was a very important discovery – we'd have no defibrillators and no Frankenstein without it – but you can feel poor Luigi's disappointment that rather than having discovered the power to bring the dead back to life, he'd merely found the power to give them a half-decent breaststroke kick.

A discovery of artefacts in Seleucia on the Tigris known collectively as the Baghdad Battery has given rise to a theory that says our old friend Mesopotamia (although in the more modern Parthian period – 250 BC–AD 224) may well, along with the wheel, writing and early breakdance pioneering, have been the source of a rudimentary battery cell. The artefacts consisted of a series of terracotta pots about 5″ tall, cylinders of rolled copper, and iron rods. If the iron rods were placed inside the copper, held in place with bitumen and then lowered into the clay pots, the pots would merely need to be filled with lemon juice or vinegar to become effective battery cells. It is thought that this might have been used for electro-plating and leaves me wondering how much digging around you would need to do in Iraq before you actually discovered a nugget of silver with a smile on its face and a ticket to 42nd Street in its hand.

ELECTRICITY

We are going to give you five clues to facts about electricity. Can you work out the answers and pick the one that you think the fewest of our 100 people knew?

A law of electromagnetic induction is named after this English scientist, born in 1791

Name of generator that uses a metal dome and a rubber belt and can make hair stand on end

Name of the green and yellow-striped wire attached to one of the pins in a plug

Negatively charged sub-atomic particles the flow of which through a wire creates an electric current

Rock group named after the abbreviations of two types of electric current

MICHAEL FARADAY	16
VAN DE GRAAFF GENERATOR	17
EARTH	66
ELECTRONS	22
AC/DC	78

41
NINETEENTH-CENTURY BOOKS

This is absolutely the type of category we reveal on the *Pointless* board to exasperated fury from all contestants. The only categories we ever reveal to greater anger are 'British Politicians' and 'Snooker'.

But it is a truly remarkable category. In terms of scope and influence the nineteenth century was the most extraordinary era for books. Sure, the eighteenth century had *Gulliver's Travels* and *Robinson Crusoe*, the twentieth century had *To Kill a Mockingbird* and *Tall, Dark and Hansen* – the autobiography of Alan Hansen – and the twenty-first century has already had *Fifty Shades of Grey*, *Fifty Shades Darker* and *Fifty Shades Freed*. But take a look at this for a top ten of books, all first published in the nineteenth century, and see if you think any other era could ever hope to compete.

10. *Dracula* by Bram Stoker
    Based on the films.

9. *Les Misérables* by Victor Hugo
   An extraordinary epic, telling the story of whether Hugh Jackman can sing or not.

8. *Jane Eyre* by Charlotte Brontë
   Every single time we do a round on nineteenth-century literature or the Brontës, I can see the same fear on everyone's faces as their brain gets 'Jane Eyre' and 'Jane Austen' mixed up, before then getting Charlotte Brontë and Emily Brontë mixed up. It's like the contestant who began panicking about the difference between J. Edgar Hoover and Herbert Hoover and ended up telling us there was once a US President called Henry Hoover.

7. *A Study in Scarlet* by Arthur Conan Doyle
   The first appearance of the greatest detective of all time, Sherlock Holmes, though this book is simply a compendium of home decoration tips.

6. *Frankenstein* by Mary Shelley
   You have to remember that 'Frankenstein' is the name of the doctor, not the name of the monster, or people on the internet get very angry with you.

5. *The Communist Manifesto* by Karl Marx
   Made famous by the TV adaptation in which Colin Firth, playing the role of the lumpen proletariat, forever denied access to ownership of the means of production, emerges dripping from a lake in a white shirt.

4. *Wuthering Heights* by Kate Bush
   Her only novel.

3. *On the Origin of Species* by Charles Darwin
   The first example of a book where all the heroes are animals. Without this book we would not have had *The Tiger Who Came for Tea, Babe: Pig in the City* or my new novel *Lord Sebastian Jacobs – The Giraffe Who Thought He Was a Rhinoceros.*

2. *Great Expectations* by Charles Dickens
   It was so hard to choose just one work by Dickens. First, because he has written so many magnificent novels, but mainly because I haven't read any of them. I have gone with the one that comes up first when you Google him.

1. *Pride and Prejudice* by Jane Austen
   Which is better, 'pride' or 'prejudice'? That is the question Austen asks us in this extraordinary *tour de force*. We know that 'prejudice' is first alphabetically, but isn't prejudice a bad thing? 'Pride' comes before a fall, but also describes a group of lions, and lions are often a good thing. Austen keeps us guessing right up until the incredible denouement, high on the cliffs above the French Riviera.

So, proof that the nineteenth century was very much the best for books of all kinds. But the twentieth century comes out on top for 'The Ten Greatest Britpop Singles' and the twenty-first century is unbeatable in '10 Cats You Won't BELIEVE Could Fall Off A Piano'.

CHARLES DARWIN

Here are five clues to facts about the scientist Charles Darwin. Can you work out which is the most obscure?

Dropped out of a medical degree at this university

Is on which denomination of Bank of England note which was first issued in 2000?

Place of worship in which he is buried

Ship in which he voyaged around the world, beginning in 1831

Town of birth

EDINBURGH	4
£10	9
WESTMINSTER ABBEY	19
HMS *BEAGLE*	34
SHREWSBURY	5

42
TELEPHONE

Alexander Graham Bell was destined to invent the telephone. Obviously. I mean, otherwise he'd have been called Alexander Graham Smith or Alexander Fruit Salad. I mean, hello (which, by the way, is a general greeting invented – or at least appropriated – for the telephone so that people speaking to each other in different time zones had a cordial opening gambit that wasn't specifically Good Morning or Good Evening). In truth, Mr Bell was really interested in speech and hearing, having a mother and wife who were both deaf. Presumably he got tired of having to scream at the top of his lungs at dinner every night and decided that if he *really* wanted the salt he was going to have to do something about it. Adversity, or in Bell's case having to yell quite a lot, really was the mother of invention.

Little did Mr Bell know that even in its first incarnation he'd in fact created the most powerful tool his mother – or indeed any mother – could possibly have. Before the invention of the telephone, the only technology by which mothers could exercise matriarchal control over children who'd left home was the Letter. The problem with the Letter, however – even the Strongly Worded Letter – was that there was no way of guaranteeing that it would be delivered just at the very moment its recipient's entire family would be sitting down for supper. This was the genius of the telephone: it harnessed the mother's instinctive telepathy to such ingenious effect that she could be sure that over 90 per cent of the time her calls would be timed with pinpoint accuracy.

Hilariously, Bell found his own invention so irritating and intrusive that he wouldn't even have a telephone in his office. Considering Bell invented the thing in the 1870s, which was some time before the first person ever even thought of alerting everyone to the possibility of a PPI rebate, you begin to realise quite how much he either prized his solitude or regretted installing a line in his mother's sitting room. What @BellCanto1847 would have made of today's mobile version of his invention, with its infinite applications, is anyone's guess. But his innovation started a connectivity revolution that would come to change the functioning of our species. Where once we were solitary beings who had to carry whatever limited expertise we could cram into our brains, we have evolved to become part of a constantly updating circuit of information, a central cloud of wisdom that we can tap into whenever we need to know something. No person now need ever be truly alone unless they want to be (or the electricity runs out). The corollary to this is that very few people are as self-sufficient as previous generations, but on the whole I think we're happy with that as a trade-off.

Alexander Graham Netflix, we salute you.

FAMOUS VICTORIANS

Here are some descriptions of famous Victorians. We have given you the initials of their names as they are most commonly known. Can you work out their names and select which one the fewest of our 100 knew?

We are defining Victorian as anyone who appears in the book *Great Victorian Lives*, which contains obituaries of the most influential Victorians as profiled by *The Times* newspaper.

A pioneer of antiseptic surgery (JL)

African explorer, found by Stanley in 1871 (DL)

Art critic who wrote *Modern Painters* (JR)

Designed Clifton Suspension Bridge (IKB)

Evolutionist who sailed on HMS *Beagle* (CD)

Father of Arts and Crafts movement 1834–96 (WM)

JOSEPH LISTER 28

DAVID LIVINGSTONE 59

JOHN RUSKIN 2

ISAMBARD KINGDOM BRUNEL 67

CHARLES DARWIN 43

WILLIAM MORRIS 25

FAMOUS VICTORIANS

Irish nationalist leader 1846–91 (CSP)

Known as the 'Lady with the Lamp' (FN)

Painted 'The Fighting Temeraire' (JMWT)

Poet who wrote *Dover Beach* (MA)

Rival of Gladstone, he was PM 1874–80 (BD)

Wrote *The Mayor of Casterbridge* (TH)

CHARLES STEWART PARNELL   8

FLORENCE NIGHTINGALE   70

JMW TURNER   23

MATTHEW ARNOLD   2

BENJAMIN DISRAELI   33

THOMAS HARDY   40

CARS

The year 1886 is generally considered to be that in which the car was born, when Karl Benz built his Patent Motorwagen. If he had decided to call it the Benz Motor Wagon, instead, he would also have invented BMW at the same time, which would have been some going. As always, lots of people had built similar contraptions earlier than this, but they weren't German so they didn't really work.

Commercially available cars took a long time to arrive, in much the same way that if you order an Uber mini-cab in South London it sometimes takes a long time to arrive. The most famous early car was Henry Ford's Model T in 1908, and his revolutionary production line was so fast that his famous quote 'any colour, as long as it's black' came from the fact that 'Japan Black' paint was the only colour that would dry quickly enough to keep up with the astonishing speed of the rest of the assembly process.

Benz sold just twenty-five of his Patent Motorwagen. In

2016, 74 million cars were sold worldwide. It is fair to say that cars caught on. So much so that within twenty years, horses had died out.

There have been some drawbacks to the rise of the automobile, including massively increased pollution, traffic jams, out-of-town retail parks, traffic wardens, people who drop their kids off at school in four-by-fours despite living five minutes' walk away, 'drivetime' DJs, an over-reliance on oil leading to prolonged global conflict, Formula 1, and people who pick their nose at traffic lights.

But cars have also brought many benefits to the world, such as the shops you get in twenty-four-hour garages. Before cars we simply would never have been able to get a Twix at two in the morning. Also, car 'Top Trumps' are the best 'Top Trumps'.

Cars truly divide us though. Statistically, the single most contentious issue in British history, the one that divides us above all others, is whether we like Jeremy Clarkson or not. I do, but please don't tell anyone.

But the car as we know it has perhaps had its day. They are ludicrously dangerous and wasteful, which is why we secretly like them so much. In the future we will all travel in 'driverless cars', which, it is hoped, will reduce our risk of accidents, reduce road congestion and reduce our exposure to discussions about the dangers of immigration.

Can you name any driver in the history of Formula One to have won at least ten Grand Prix races? This is up to the end of the 2012 season. As ever, we are looking for the most obscure answer.

Please note that this list does not include Nico Rosberg who has won over ten Grand Prix races since this question was asked to our 100 people.

ALAIN PROST	23	JENSON BUTTON	23
ALAN JONES	0	JIM CLARK	7
ALBERTO ASCARI	3	JODY SCHECKTER	1
AYRTON SENNA	36	JUAN MANUEL FANGIO	14
CARLOS REUTEMANN	0	KIMI RÄIKKÖNEN	4
DAMON HILL	19	LEWIS HAMILTON	28
DAVID COULTHARD	3	MARIO ANDRETTI	0
EMERSON FITTIPALDI	3	MICHAEL SCHUMACHER	55
FELIPE MASSA	3	MIKA HÄKKINEN	4
FERNANDO ALONSO	9	NELSON PIQUET	3
GERHARD BERGER	1	NIGEL MANSELL	26
GRAHAM HILL	18	NIKI LAUDA	9
JACK BRABHAM	4	RONNIE PETERSON	0
JACKIE STEWART	22	RUBENS BARRICHELLO	1
JACQUES VILLENEUVE	0	SEBASTIAN VETTEL	6
JAMES HUNT	15	STIRLING MOSS	32

44
WRIGHT BROTHERS FLY

The actual journey on that auspicious day of 13 December 1903, when the Wright brothers finally achieved controlled powered flight, was over a distance of 852 feet. This was an epochal achievement but admittedly didn't do much to add to their Air Miles account. The plane was called *Flyer I*, which although singularly unpoetic at least showed confidence that there would be (or tacit admission that there'd need to be, depending on your perspective) a *Flyer II*, which – spoiler alert – there was. The main reason for the *Flyer II* project was not so much to make improvements to *Flyer I* but to make sure that enough people were watching. *Flyer I* had been followed by a lengthy process during which the brothers, having attained one of the most significant transportational goals in the human story so far, had to travel around talking about their great achievement to roomfuls of eminent people shouting 'chinny re-ckon' at them. This, one imagines, must have been frustrating. Although also understandable. If a couple of brothers, one of whom was called 'Orville', started lecturing tomorrow about how they'd successfully pioneered teleportation, I would be sceptical if they didn't have proof.

The Wright brothers' main mistake, it would appear, was in not waiting for the age of mass television before making their first flight attempt, as a nice documentary with Maggie Philbin and footage of *Flyer I* would have silenced a lot of doubters. It would also mean, given the delayed start of aviation, we would probably know where Amelia Earhart was; though possibly not *who* she was, so maybe actually we wouldn't really care that much after all.

The Wrights also gave us the first fatal plane crash in 1908, in which a young army lieutenant was killed and Orville Wright was lucky to escape with his life. This ended an exemplary safety record but happily it didn't kill off enthusiasm for flight. Not only would Amelia Earhart have had to take up long-distance sailing to pull a, frankly, attention-seeking mid-Pacific disappearing act but the seminal 1960s pop song 'Leaving on a Jet Plane' by Peter, Paul and Mary would never have been released. Such things are too hideous a loss to our shared cultural heritage even to contemplate. On the bright side, no-one would ever have heard of Michael O'Leary.

Thankfully, many incredible technological aviation innovations have been forthcoming since the Wright brothers' magnificent achievement, including rotating baggage carousels and Leon Restaurants now at a number of British terminals. Yes, it truly is a brave, new – and much *smaller* – world thanks to Orville and Wilbur Wright.

FLIGHTS AND FLYING MACHINES

We are going to give you five clues to facts about flights and flying machines. We would like you to tell us the answer to the fact you think the fewest of our 100 people knew.

A form of rigid airship named after a German count and used to bomb Britain during the First World War

The century in which the first nonstop solo aeroplane flight across the Atlantic was made

Nickname of the flying boat designed by Howard Hughes that flew just once in 1947

Supersonic passenger plane that ceased flying in 2003

Surname of the aviation pioneers Wilbur and Orville

ZEPPELIN	44
20TH CENTURY	56
SPRUCE GOOSE	17
CONCORDE	89
WRIGHT	62

TELEVISION!

The first ever public demonstration of television, as we would come to know it, was made by John Logie Baird in Selfridge's London department store on 25 March 1925. It was a moving, talking silhouette of a ventriloquist's dummy called 'Stucky Bill'. Stucky Bill went on to host *The One Show* and *Look East* before drinking himself into rehab, contracting chronic woodworm and releasing an autobiography called *Keeping My Hand In*.

In less than a hundred years from this moment, television has become the single most popular, most successful, most influential, most varied and most ubiquitous art form in the history of mankind.

Even more amazingly, though, no-one knows how television actually works. John Logie Baird forgot to tell anyone, and after he'd died it was too late. He was very like Colonel Sanders in that regard. The most we can do therefore is guess how it works, so here is my attempt to explain the process.

Where *Pointless* is concerned we sit in a studio and cameras are pointed at us. At this stage we are real people and we say real things. The podiums are made of some sort of MDF painted silver to look like metal, as is my desk. But if you were there you could actually touch stuff. Except Xander – never touch Xander. The camera that is always pointing at me (in case I do a pun about a horse or whatever I do) is camera six, and that is usually operated by Leila. The images go into Leila's camera and then through a wire into a 'gallery' where they join all the pictures from all the other cameras.

What happens next? Well, there are a number of buttons in the gallery and someone has to press these while simultaneously saying things like 'mid-shot on three please Clare' and 'lighting state two please Tom'. If they do this correctly, and they are able to drink coffee and eat Haribo or 'Miniature Heroes' and gossip about the people who do the same job as them on *The Chase*, then a TV programme comes out the other end.

This 'programme', which is about seventy minutes long and includes footage you can't show on television, such as me and Xander accidentally swearing, or the pointless column repeatedly breaking down, is then put on a computer disk and taken into an edit suite.

What happens next? Well, there are even more buttons in the edit suite, with different people saying things like 'do we have podium three on iso here?' and 'do we have a version of this where Richard manages to pronounce

"Lesotho" correctly'? There is more coffee, more Haribo and more gossiping about the people who work in the edit suites on *Tipping Point*. At the end of this process we have a forty-five-minute show.

This then goes to the BBC and they check it is broadcastable, which at least 30 per cent of the time it is. It is now ready to be 'television'. And how does that happen?

Well, magic, pretty much. It goes from a computer somewhere in the BBC through wires or waves into the TV you bought last year and which, if you're honest, is slightly too big for that wall but you're refusing to admit it. You watch it as if we are really tiny and actually in your house, but really we are just made of electricity and dots. When I walk down a residential street around teatime I often see people watching *Pointless* and I cannot begin to tell you how tempted I am to wander up to their house, knock on their window and wave. One day I will.

When *Pointless* is finished the *News* is on. I cannot speak for Sophie Raworth or Huw Edwards personally but, again, I believe they are not really inside your television set. The only person who definitely is inside your television set is Dale Winton, who always has this written into his contracts.

And that's television. If you have any more questions please press the Red Button, however that works.

TELEVISION FAMILIES

We are going to give you the first names of members of fourteen fictional television families. Can you provide the surname of the family in each instance, and work out which one the fewest of our 100 people knew?

Arthur, Pauline, Michelle, Mark and Martin

Caleb, Shadrach, Zak, Ezra and Albert

Cathy, Dermot, Mark, Rory and Bono

Fred, Wilma and Pebbles

Homer, Marge, Lisa, Bart and Maggie

Jim, Paul, Julie, Scott and Lucy

JR, Sue Ellen and John Ross

FOWLER	56	*EASTENDERS*
DINGLE	29	*EMMERDALE*
BROWN	15	*MRS BROWN'S BOYS*
FLINTSTONE	94	*THE FLINTSTONES*
SIMPSON	88	*THE SIMPSONS*
ROBINSON	20	*NEIGHBOURS*
EWING	60	*DALLAS*

TELEVISION FAMILIES

Nellie, Joey, Jack, Adrian, Aveline and Billy

Pam, Mick and Gavin

Peter, Lois, Chris, Meg and Stewie

Richard, Hyacinth and Sheridan

Sebastian, Julia and Cordelia

Tony, Carmela, Meadow and AJ

Walter, Skyler and Walt Jnr

BOSWELL	11	*BREAD*
SHIPMAN	4	*GAVIN AND STACEY*
GRIFFIN	18	*FAMILY GUY*
BUCKET	70	*KEEPING UP APPEARANCES*
FLYTE	2	*BRIDESHEAD REVISITED*
SOPRANO	4	*THE SOPRANOS*
WHITE	4	*BREAKING BAD*

46
CHURCHILL

Not being much of a historian – and not having been around during the Second World War – I thought I would ask my father-in-law for his thoughts on Churchill just to see if there was anything I could add to the usual cannon of *bon mots* and school history book nuggets. My father-in-law took a deep breath and spoke for several minutes. Here is a verbatim account of what he said:

Winston Churchill was one of the most disastrous military leaders in English history. Misled by his early experiences as a junior officer – moonlighting as a journalist, as you'll remember* – he confidently assumed responsibilities he was quite unfitted to discharge.

In 1916 he committed British and Australian forces – of course supported by the now-forgotten French – to taking on the Turks at Gallipoli. Big mistake. They were soundly

* I nodded vigorously, *but didn't . . .*

beaten and the Allies were forced to withdraw humiliated while the English earned the undying hatred of the Australians and New Zealanders – albeit the quizzical admiration of the Turks. This is actually a good example of three of Churchill's chief characteristics as a military leader: a belief that the enemy was best attacked as indirectly as possible, a tendency to irritate his allies, and an inability to think things through.

One thing Churchill did not lack, though, was courage; after the Dardanelles disaster he went off to the trenches of the Western front as a lieutenant-colonel – bitterly disappointed not to be made a general – a fact for which those he would have commanded I should think must have been very grateful.

But his military judgement never showed any signs of improvement. His Chief of Staff, Alanbrooke, thought that Churchill constituted the single most important obstacle to the efficient deployment of forces in the Second World War. He disliked [Field Marshal] Montgomery, who with [Field Marshal] Slim were the only really successful battle commanders in the war against the Germans and Japanese, and believed that [Field Marshal] Alexander was largely responsible for Montgomery's defeat of Rommel.

Churchill's address to the British commanders before the 1944 invasion of Normandy was so dispiriting with its criticisms of the constitution of the British forces that Montgomery had to take him on one side and ask him if he would like to run the show himself. Churchill favoured the invasion of Sumatra instead.

Paradoxically, it was this incompetence, allied with a gift for a public rhetoric just this side of the ridiculous, that secured his place in history. In May 1940 it was clear to every properly informed person that the war against Germany was lost. The Duke of Windsor, the former King Edward VIII, was passing military secrets to the enemy; the Germans, don't forget, allied with the Soviet Union and the Italians, had occupied France, most of Scandinavia, Austria and Poland. The British Army was about to be driven into the sea at Dunkirk. A very large proportion of British fighter pilots were foreigners. But in five days, Churchill managed to outmanoeuvre those who, like Halifax and other Tory Party leaders, were prepared to come to terms with the Nazis, rallied the country and declared that, under no circumstances, would the British accept terms from Hitler.

Until then he had been self-absorbed, vain, politically unreliable and generally unpopular. But in May 1940 he achieved greatness. He saved Britain from the psychological disaster of collaboration with one of the most evil men in world history, and spared several generations of his countrymen from the wounded hypocrisy and false faith of Britain's European neighbours.

His refusal to accept defeat was in principle insane. But his contribution to the welfare of his country was immeasurable. Never in the field of human conflict has so much been owed to someone of such little understanding.

What else do you want to know?

The only other thing I know about Churchill is that he ended all his conversations with Franklin D. Roosevelt by saying 'KBO, KBO', which Roosevelt was baffled by but too polite to question. When he eventually asked an aide what on earth it meant, he was told that 'Keep Buggering On' was a favourite sign-off of the PM.

RAF AIRCRAFT
DURING THE SECOND WORLD WAR

Here are five anagrams which, when solved, will give the names of RAF Aircraft in use during the Second World War. We would like you to unscramble the anagrams and tell us the names of the aircraft.

In each case, we've given the common short-form names of the aircraft.

A RADAR CUB

GOLD TIARA

QUITS MOO

RAUNCHIER

RIPE FIST

BARRACUDA	6
GLADIATOR	1
MOSQUITO	58
HURRICANE	21
SPITFIRE	68

1970

Both Xander and I were born in the year 1970. I was born in a small shed near Billericay in Essex, surrounded by striking Ford workers, Xander on a crimson throne in a secret hollowed-out volcano, attended to by the Archbishop of Canterbury, the Queen and a young Moira Stuart (citation needed).

So how has the world changed since 1970?

Well, first the average British house price in 1970 was £4,950. In parts of Billericay that has nearly doubled since then.

A loaf of bread cost 9 pence. A loaf of organic sourdough artisanal rosemary and cumin seed focaccia didn't exist. Neither did quinoa, sushi, oven chips, Nando's, Mint Viennetta, UKIP, *Tipping Point*, stuffed-crust pizza, McNuggets, TripAdvisor, *Grand Theft Auto V* or dogging. Different times.

A pint of lager cost 20 pence and a bottle of wine £1. Britain in 1970 was essentially like France today.

The Range Rover was launched in 1970, at a cost of £1,998. I've just looked it up and it will now cost you over £81,750. The only people who can afford Range Rovers these days are footballers, Prince Philip and Bradley Walsh.

A trip for two to the cinema cost just 90 pence. I've just looked that up too and that will also now cost you £81,750, though that includes a regular Coke and a bag of Revels.

In 1970 Mick Jagger was fined £200 for possession of marijuana. This certainly had the desired effect, as Mick hasn't taken any drugs since, and the music business as a whole is now pretty much narcotic free. Our drug laws work.

The Beatles, very much the One Direction of 1970, split up. The first to leave was Paul McCartney, very much the Zayn Malik of 1970. Expect Zayn to release his version of 'The Frog Chorus' sometime around 2028. Also, get your money on Harry Styles narrating *Thomas the Tank Engine*.

Richard Branson launched the Virgin group in 1970. It was due to be launched in 1968 but was delayed due to signalling problems in the Peterborough area.

Deaths in 1970 included Bertrand Russell, Charles de Gaulle (one of the few men ever named after an airport), Sonny Liston, E. M. Forster, Jimi Hendrix and Gypsy Rose Lee. These fine folk were directly replaced in 1970 by me, Xander, Tina Fey, Mariah Carey, Zoe Ball and Andi Peters.

Prince Charles joined the navy, safe in the knowledge that in a few short years he would be king.

THE 1970s

We are going to give you twelve clues to people and events relating to the 1970s. Please give us the answers.

Art historian who was revealed as the 'fourth man' in 1979

British male golfer who won the US Open in 1970

Chilean President overthrown in a military coup led by Augusto Pinochet in 1973

Common name given to Communist Party that ruled Cambodia (1975–9)

Country that seceded from Pakistan in 1971

Egyptian who succeeded Nasser as President in 1970

ANTHONY BLUNT 16

TONY JACKLIN 14

SALVADOR ALLENDE 4

KHMER ROUGE 22

BANGLADESH 21

ANWAR SADAT 7

THE 1970s

Exiled cleric who returned to Iran in 1979 and became political and religious leader for life

General who seized power in Uganda in 1971

Name of Prime Minister of Rhodesia when it declared itself a republic in 1970

Name of the revolutionary group that overthrew the government of Nicaragua in 1979

Prime Minister who was in power during the UK's 'Winter of Discontent'

The second and third of the disputes known as the 'Cod Wars' occurred between the UK and this nation

AYATOLLAH KHOMEINI   16

IDI AMIN   32

IAN SMITH   20

SANDINISTA NATIONAL LIBERATION FRONT   3

JAMES CALLAGHAN   15

ICELAND   32

48
POINTLESS

We started making *Pointless* in 2009. Just thirty of them. The crew, the make-up team and wardrobe had all worked together on Jasper Carrott's *Golden Balls* so they all knew each other, and they'd all done plenty of one-off pilot series of game shows that had disappeared into the TV ether, so nobody was under any illusions about *Pointless*. Except me. I was under a big comfy twelve-tog, Hungarian goose-down illusion; I thought *Pointless* was ace. Between every round (and there used to be hundreds of rounds because we had so many pairs it was like a Moonie wedding) I would tell Richard that we'd be doing *Pointless* for the next hundred years and he would look at me wearily and point out that in a 'best case scenario' we would get to do sixty *Pointless* shows and that would be very much it. Richard has worked in television all his life; he knows what's what. There's no arguing with that kind of seasoned pro. Nonetheless, it didn't deter me.

Possibly because we didn't know how long we'd be riding

this particular bus, we were quick to establish some *Pointless* customs that are now, nearly 1,200 shows in, well and truly bedded in. Every time the theme music plays at the top of the show, I bang out the same rhythm on my podium, and Richard and I look at each other on the first brass stab and elbow the air behind us. Every time I say goodbye at the end of each show I close my eyes and nod my head – a thing I lifted directly from Bill Giles the weatherman of my childhood, who did exactly the same and whose mesmerising ways with a farewell I'd always admired. Backstage, in make-up and wardrobe, for no reason I can remember, we all speak in Irish accents. On set, for no reason I can remember, we often speak in broad Liverpudlian accents.

Richard was right. In our second series (another run of thirty shows) our viewing figures seemed to plateau at an okay but not dazzling level. It looked as though we were coming to the end of our best-case scenario. And then, suddenly, something extraordinary happened. In the last two weeks of the run (and when we filmed it we had to do two potential endings for the series: one saying a final goodbye-thanks-for-watching, the other saying thanks-for-watching-see-you-next-series) there was a miraculous but steady lift in the figures. Then, in the last week, Stephen Fry tweeted that he never missed an episode, and suddenly we were ON. The BBC came back and asked for sixty more shows and as a result Richard and I now get to swing our elbows up to 210 times a year.

FOUR-LETTER WORDS THAT CAN BE MADE FROM THE LETTERS P.O.I.N.T.L.E.S.S.

We are looking for any four-letter word defined in the *Oxford Dictionary of English* that can be formed using four of the letters contained in the word 'Pointless'. As ever, we will not accept trademarks, acronyms, abbreviations, proper nouns, nor vulgar words – this is a family book after all.

The answers include four-letter words that are plurals if the singular is in the *Oxford Dictionary of English*.

We are not including the word 'Less' which is way too obvious for *Pointless*.

EONS	0	NETS	5
INTO	10	NILS	0
IONS	0	NIPS	12
ISLE	7	NITE	2
LEIS	0	NITS	11
LENO	0	NOEL	3
LENS	4	NOES	0
LENT	27	NOIL	0
LEST	16	NOPE	7
LETS	8	NOSE	9
LIEN	1	NOTE	20
LIES	0	OILS	5
LINE	14	OLÉS	0
LINO	0	ONES	1
LINT	48	OPEN	9
LION	10	OPES	0
LIPS	7	OPTS	1
LISP	5	PEIN	0
LIST	19	PELT	11
LITE	3	PENS	12
LITS	1	PENT	20
LOIN	20	PEON	0
LONE	4	PESO	0
LOPE	6	PEST	28
LOPS	1	PETS	12
LOSE	11	PIES	3
LOSS	17	PILE	19
LOST	19	PINE	19
LOTI	0	PINS	32
LOTS	5	PINT	72
NESS	4	PION	0
NEST	14	PITS	9

Word	Value	Word	Value
PLIÉ	0	SNIP	13
PLOT	6	SNIT	0
POET	4	SNOT	4
POIS	0	SOIL	12
POLE	22	SOLE	15
POLS	0	SOLI	0
PONE	1	SOLS	0
PONS	0	SONE	1
PONT	10	SONS	3
POSE	13	SOPS	1
POST	19	SOTS	1
POTS	19	SPIN	16
PSIS	0	SPIT	14
PSST	0	SPOT	14
SEIS	0	STEP	13
SENT	27	STOP	19
SEPT	0	TENS	8
SETS	5	TIES	1
SILO	4	TILE	22
SILT	15	TINE	16
SINE	4	TINS	21
SINS	10	TIPS	9
SIPE	0	TOES	0
SIPS	6	TOIL	14
SITE	9	TOLE	3
SITS	0	TONE	20
SLIP	11	TONS	12
SLIT	16	TOPE	3
SLOE	1	TOPI	0
SLOP	12	TOPS	10
SLOT	9	TOSS	20

49
TODAY

More will happen today than happened in the entire first millennium. Let's just think about that for a moment.

Now let's just acknowledge that I made it up. It's probably just something I read on an HSBC advert as I was about to get on a plane. It might even be true for all I know if 'things happening' is something you measure in man-hours (person-hours? I can't believe hours haven't yet been made gender neutral – I've been watching and we both *definitely* do them) but the picture of the Inuit man in the Andean hat, sitting outside the wigwam with the iPad that would surely accompany it, would probably distract me from thinking about it too much. That and the fact that I'm getting on a plane and a tiny part of me is busy drowning out the even tinier part of me that thinks I'm never going to see terra firma – let alone that bit of it populated by either Inuit men in incongruous headgear or advertising executives – again.

Today, though, is a fabulous time to be alive. We have nearly all of us dodged conscription to fight in trenches or on beaches, we have lived through the age of antibiotics (a miraculous if short era during which we were invincible against all but a tiny handful of pathogens), we have lived in a time when heating and food have been relatively plentiful, the weather has been by and large clement, and the absence of local earthquakes and volcanic activity has kept our horizons safe, our skies clear and our populace generally uncovered by mountains of pyroclastic ash. We have the best of everything, our culture has expanded to include the young and old, we can have Benjamin Britten *and* Kanye West, Agrippa *and* Anish Kapoor, John Keats *and* John Niven. We can fly to very hot or very cold places, we can stay in touch with all our old friends while making stacks of new ones we don't necessarily have to meet. Today is a wonderful, soft, comfortable, bright, fertile, sweet-smelling, peaceful, happy and considerate time to be alive. It's not a Utopia, not by a long chalk, it's riven with injustices* but of all the many periods we have looked at in this pell-mell gad through our history, it is the one I would choose to live in every time.

Tomorrow will be the last yesterday you regret.†

---

* An example chosen at random: Timothy Dalton, through no fault of his own, had to make *Licence to Kill*, the worst Bond script of the whole Canon, and the mighty actor of *The Living Daylights*, thus tainted, never got behind that wheel again.

† Yes, I definitely made that one up – not even HSBC would touch that.

We are looking for any act that has a single which featured in the list of top 100 best-selling singles of the 21st century from January 2000 until the chart was released by the BBC on 7 May 2012.

Where two or more artists have collaborated on a single, the names of the artists will be treated as separate answers.

However, if the song is credited to a band, we are not looking for the individual band members, unless they are on the list in their own right.

Adele	22	DJ Ötzi	0
Afrojack	0	Drake	0
Akon	0	Duffy	1
Alexandra Burke	1	Ed Sheeran	0
Alicia Keys	0	Ellie Goulding	0
All Saints	0	Eminem	0
Atomic Kitten	0	Enrique Iglesias	1
B.o.B	0	Flor Rida	0
Baha Men	0	Gareth Gates	1
Band Aid 20	3	Gareth Malone	0
Beyoncé Knowles	7	Gary Jules	0
Bob the Builder	0	Girls Aloud	3
Bruno Mars	1	Gnarls Barkley	0
Calvin Harris	1	Goonrock	0
Cee Lo Green	0	Gotye	0
Cheryl Cole	1	Hayley Williams	0
Christina Aguilera	1	Hear'Say	0
Christina Perri	1	James Blunt	0
Coldplay	7	James Morrison	0
D Cup	0	Jay-Z	0
David Guetta	0	Jennifer Lopez	1

Jessie J	2	Nelly	1
Joe McElderry	0	Nelly Furtado	0
Journey	0	Ne-Yo	0
Katy Perry	0	Nickelback	0
Kelly Rowland	0	One Direction	3
Kesha	0	Owl City	0
Killers	0	Peter Kay	0
Kimbra	0	Pitbull	0
Kings of Leon	2	Rage Against the Machine	0
Kylie Minogue	7		
La Roux	0	Rihanna	14
Labrinth	0	Rikrok	0
Lady Gaga	10	Robbie Williams	24
Lauren Bennett	0	S Club 7	0
Leona Lewis	1	Shaggy	1
LMFAO	0	Shakira	0
Maroon 5	1	Shayne Ward	2
Matt Cardle	0	Sia	0
Michael Andrews	0	Snoop Dogg	0
Military Wives	0	Snow Patrol	0
Nayer	0	Sonique	0

Taio Cruz	0	Wheatus	0
Take That	25	Will Young	1
The Black Eyed Peas	2	Will.I.am	2
Tinie Tempah	0	Wyclef Jean	0
Tony Christie	0	X Factor Finalists	0
Usher	0	Yolanda Be Cool	0
Westlife	7		

50 TOMORROW

So what have we learned during our dubious spin through history? What can we keep with us as we stumble into the future?

Well, essentially we are all still the same people who painted on cave walls, who struck flints to create sparks, who protected their tribes from the unknown tribe in the next valley, who worshipped the sun that rose and feared the sun that fell. We are all still Mesopotamians, we are all still Picts fighting the Romans or Romans fighting the Picts, we continue to write our Domesday Books, we are all still Wat Tyler and Anne Boleyn, we're still plotting to advance our cause with gunpowder, or accidentally starting fires on Pudding Lane. We're writing dictionaries and improving engines and building shelters and protecting our families.

Great empires all crumble, pursuit of power is a folly, ideas of 'progress', of the world working towards some form of conclusion, are a myth. Our technology 'advances' as we build on the shoulders of others, but doesn't make us happier. Our thinking 'advances' as we attempt to learn the lessons of history, but we are no nearer to actually agreeing with each other about anything.

One day our entire lives, all the things we hold dear, all the things we rally against, all the things we fear, will just be a page of text in a book. That's the lot of the human race.

And one day it will all be gone. Maybe an asteroid will do for us like it did for the dinosaurs, maybe a plague, maybe our endless 'progress' will heat the planet up so much our story will simply fizzle out.

But, by God, what luck we've had to have lived at all. To see the beauty we see, to hear the jokes, to dance to the music, to hug, to love, simply to be.

We only have one job tomorrow. To leave the world a slightly better place than we found it. Ring your mum, be kind to animals, be proud of yourself and be understanding of others. Everything else is pointless.

DYSTOPIAN NOVELS

We're going to give you the title and year of publication of fourteen famous dystopian novels or novellas, that is, the all-present bleak visions of the future. In each case, we'd like you to identify the author, please.

A Clockwork Orange (1962)

Brave New World (1932)

Do Androids Dream of Electric Sheep? (1968)

Fahrenheit 451 (1953)

Lord of the Flies (1954)

Never Let Me Go (2005)

Nineteen Eighty-Four (1949)

ANTHONY BURGESS	6
ALDOUS HUXLEY	33
PHILIP K. DICK	2
RAY BRADBURY	8
WILLIAM GOLDING	16
KAZUO ISHIGURO	0
GEORGE ORWELL	53

DYSTOPIAN NOVELS

The Children of Men (1992)

The Day of the Triffids (1951)

The Handmaid's Tale (1985)

The Hunger Games (2008)

The Road (2006)

The Running Man (1982)

The Time Machine (1895)

P. D. JAMES	1
JOHN WYNDHAM	22
MARGARET ATWOOD	2
SUZANNE COLLINS	6
CORMAC MCCARTHY	1
STEPHEN KING	4
H. G. WELLS	42